The Wisdom
of Water

For Sufi,
    Let the wisdom
    Flow
    and the love
    fall like rain.
        Adam
        06/1

John Archer was born in Toowoomba, Queensland in 1941. His twenty-one books, lectures, seminars and radio programs reflect his various passions, which include building, architecture, transport, the failures of modern medicine and, since 1990, water. His most recent book is *Twenty Thirst Century*. He lives in an old cottage on the edge of the forest, surrounded by mermaids and rainbow lorikeets.

His website is: www.johnarcher.com.au

# The Wisdom of Water

### JOHN ARCHER

inspired LIVING

**ALLEN&UNWIN**

First published in 2008

Inspired Living, an imprint of
Allen & Unwin
83 Alexander Street
Crows Nest NSW 2065
Australia
Phone:    (61 2) 8425 0100
Fax:      (61 2) 9906 2218
Email:    info@allenandunwin.com
Web:      www.allenandunwin.com

National Library of Australia
Cataloguing-in-Publication entry:

Archer, John, 1941–
The wisdom of water

ISBN 978 1 74175 239 7

Water–Folklore. Water–Mythology. Water–Religious aspects.
Water and civilisation. Mysticism.

398.364

pp. 58, 107, 131 and 179: from *Net of Fireflies*, translated by Harold Stewart, © 1960 by Harold Stewart. Used by permission of Tuttle Publishing.

pp. 63–4: from *Rolling Thunder* by Douglas Boyd, © 1974 by Robert Briggs Assoc. Used by permission of Random House, Inc.

pp. 176–7: from *Ceremony* by Leslie Marmon Silko, © 1977 by Leslie Silko. Used by permission of Viking Penguin, a division of Penguin Group (USA) Inc.

pp. 279–280: from *Nature as Teacher* by Viktor Schauberger, translated and edited by Callum Coats. Used by kind permission of Gill & Macmillan Ltd for Gateway Books.

p. 335: from *The English Writings of Rabindranath Tagore*, Volume I, Poems, 1994. Used by kind permission of the Sahitya Akademi.

Illustrations by Lisa White
Text design by Christabella Designs
Typeset in 12/16pt Bembo by Midland Typesetters, Australia
Printed in Australia by Ligare Book Printer, Sydney

10 9 8 7 6 5 4 3 2 1

Through water flows the
wisdom of the universe.
Is it not this wisdom
itself which has created the
element of water as a
tool for its own creativity?

Theodor Schwenk *Sensitive Chaos*

# Contents

# The Treasure House of Innumerable Secrets

'Because water has such great powers of absorption and conservation it is a treasure house of innumerable secrets. The whole of the history of mankind is recorded in the rivers, lakes and oceans of the world, for everything leaves traces of its existence, and the traces of all beings, all objects and all events live on in the water...

It is the supreme magic medium which permeates and impregnates the universe. If you know how to listen to a drop of water it will speak to you...'

Omraam Mikhaël Aïvanhov
*The Mysteries of Fire and Water*

Water—we turn on our taps and there it is—reliable and abundant. No wonder we take it for granted. Water is an essential part of our daily life. We drink it, cook with it, wash our bodies and our possessions in it. We use water to nourish our gardens, to quench fires and cool buildings by humidifying air. Then we swim in it for relaxation.

Water is an essential solvent and coolant in industrial and chemical processes, flowing and dripping through manufacturing plants to mould, blend, rinse and cleanse. It takes around 200,000 litres of water to produce a modern car and 8000 to put a kilo of mince on your table—and so on.

You've heard it all before.

Over and over again we are told how much our future well-being and prosperity depend on this 'our most precious resource'. Environmental scientists, hydrologists and economists refer to water and the natural world as resources whose sole function is to provide 'environmental services' to humans.

This mechanistic view of nature has been responsible for a great deal of thoughtless destruction.

To me the word 'resource' is as emotionally laden as 'ethnic cleansing'. When we refer to water or forests or animals or humans as resources, we deny them their identity, individuality and spirituality. Resources are passive. They need 'sustainable management' so that we can continue to extract the maximum 'yield' from them.

But when we love someone or something they cease to be a resource. Would you describe your mother as a resource? Your lover, your children, the family pet—are they resources?

The words we use to describe things determine our attitude to them. If we want to change that we have to expand our vocabulary, and our consciousness.

I, too, used to think of water as a resource until I came to know it more intimately.

That was twenty years ago.

Now water is my principal source of spiritual nourishment and the focus of my daily religious practice. Water is my teacher, my inspiration, consolation, lover and friend.

How does that work in practice you might ask? I'll give you an example:

Many of my early books were conceived and written in a tiny three-roomed goldminer's cabin overlooking Mallacoota Lake in Victoria's Gippsland. Each time I arrived I'd set up the same old wooden worktable at the same corner window which gave an expansive view of the water, and here I'd write for twelve or fourteen hours a day. There was a small dinghy moored at the jetty. If I needed to think I'd row out into the lake and just sit. Sometimes I'd row for miles until I was tired, come back, sleep for a while, then wake up refreshed and ready to return to writing.

One night when the waning moon hung low in the sky, I rowed out into the middle of the silent lake, shipped the oars and drifted, bathed in golden light. The boat gently rose and fell as if it rested on the breast of a living breathing entity. I stood because I could no longer sit in the presence of such beauty. Tears of joy or bliss ran down my cheeks. The sound of some night bird floated across the water and into my open heart. I sat down, wrapping my shawl around me. Hours passed unnoticed, until the sun rose and I rowed slowly home, filled with a renewed sense of connection and purpose.

This is how water speaks to us, not in words, but directly to the spirit, and somehow we feel uplifted without knowing why, without even wanting to know why. Listening to the rhythm of the ocean waves or the gurgle of a mountain stream or the sound of falling water, we can hear the voice of the Divine Intelligence. In its presence we need do nothing but *be* in the fullest sense of the word and, in its own time, water will communicate with us.

In 1922 D.H. Lawrence wrote: 'Water is $H_2O$, hydrogen two parts, oxygen one, but there is a third thing that makes it water, and nobody knows what it is'. What is this mysterious third thing Lawrence speaks of?

Could it be spirit?

The Cogui people live in the high forests of the snow-capped Andes Mountains in Columbia. Remote from civilisation they have kept their religion and way of life intact for uncounted millennia. The Cogui scriptures begin with the question, 'What is water?' The answer is that water is a living conscious entity that thinks and feels. A stream is a baby, a river an adult, the ocean is the Great All-powerful One. In the language of the Cogui the word 'creation' translates as 'water-thinking'.

What if, as the Cogui believe, this earth we inhabit is water's intentional creation, a process which began when the planet was just a spinning molten core? Could water really have created the universe and shaped the planet we inhabit? Could water be Chi, Prana, the Great Tao—the spirit that animates and manifests itself in all things? Is that possible?

When I was a child I was told that God made the world. Now scientists tell me that the world made itself, which begs the question, how exactly?

How did the Earth bring itself into being? The short answer is that the Earth is water's creation.

The water within and around us came from

somewhere out there in the universe and, for some reason known only to itself, it chose this spinning molten ball to enclose in its cooling mist. For uncounted millions of years water was the only living thing on earth. And this same water has been circulating through the earth ever since—through every bird, animal, tree and rock. It has been everywhere, seen everything.

'The same stream of life that runs through my veins night and day runs through the world and dances in rhythmic measures', writes the Indian mystic Rabindrath Tagore. Within us too the moonstruck tides ebb and flow, the sea inside moves in concert with the ocean beyond, affecting our senses and emotions, our reactions and responses. These 'rushing sea tides of the soul' open our hearts like oysters to the moon.

Through the medium of water we are connected, not only to the moon and the cosmos, but to all living things past and present. If water retains within its structure the memory of its history, then it is indeed a consciousness beyond our imagining.

Because of this cosmic connection some esoteric philosophers assert that every drop of water contains the recollection of everything that ever was and ever has been, the collective memory of the universe known as the *Chronicles of the Akasha*. It is not by chance that the word 'memory' has its origins in *mem*, the ancient Hebrew designation for water.

The desire of humans to communicate with the divinity of water led to the evolution of water gods and goddesses who surface in the myths, legends, parables and scriptures of all cultures. Ceremonies and rituals evolved around these powerful deities who could bestow life and abundance by their presence or by their absence, death and famine.

As we become increasingly aware of our dependence on fresh water for our survival, there is a resurgence of interest in the spiritual aspect of our relationship. That is as it should be. But our prayers for rain are meaningless unless they are accompanied by a recognition that nature is conscious; that because animals, plants, earth and water respond to love and respect, our thoughts and intentions have a significant impact on the environment around us. In this context love is the unconditional acceptance of the natural world as a spiritually alive and conscious entity; it is through that love that we experience the unity that connects us to the Divine.

The first step then, if we wish to enter the Treasure House of Innumerable Secrets, is to acknowledge that water is alive. This means laying aside some preconditioned 'scientific' ideas about the world, and going direct to the Source.

'Go to the pine if you want to learn about the pine or the bamboo if you want to learn about the bamboo,' the Zen master Basho instructed his pupils. 'And in doing so you must leave behind your subjective preoccupation with yourself. Otherwise you impose yourself on the subject and do not learn.' This is how we allow nature to reveal itself to us, by emptying ourselves and allowing the spirit of the water and the forest to fill that space.

But first you must empty your cup in order to be able to listen like a child hearing the stories that follow for the very first time.

A famous Zen teaching parable tells how a learned professor of religious studies came to visit an old Zen master, eager to hear what gems of wisdom the great man might have to offer.

'Sit down' said the master, graciously bowing to his guest, 'and let us have some tea.' Setting a small porcelain cup in front of the professor, the master leant across and began to pour fragrant green *sencha* from an exquisite pot. Both watched the cup slowly fill, then overflow, gradually spreading across the top of the lacquered table. The master didn't register any emotion. He just kept pouring.

'Stop' shouted the astonished professor as a trickle of hot tea flowed off the table and into his lap. 'Stop— the cup is overflowing!'

'Exactly,' said the master, 'and you are like this cup, full of your own ideas and preconceptions, feelings and emotions. Unless you empty yourself of these, how can new knowledge ever be gained?'

With my empty cup I kept company with streams and rivers, sat beneath cascades of crystal, made pilgrimages to holy springs and healing waters, slept in houseboats rocked by gentle waves. I revelled in the beauty of the rainbow and the majesty of cloud-filled sunsets. I made love in the early morning dew and was mesmerised by the reflection of the moon on the rippling waves of the ocean. On my lifelong journey back to the Source I've fallen under the influence of Stoics and Sufis, Taoists, Zen poet monks and Lamas, whose teachings illuminated my path and showed me the Way.

Now my cup overflows with the stories, poems, parables, myths and legends that have spread themselves over the pages of this book. I've arranged them under headings like Snow, Dew, Ice, Rainbows, etc. These are just some of the many manifestations of water that merit closer attention.

This is not a book to hurry through. Relax, take your time. Put it down when you've finished a chapter and think about it.

*The Wisdom of Water* offers you an opportunity to immerse yourself in water's mysteries, to explore its hidden depths and expand your experience, so that you can look up at the clouds with new eyes and hear the voice of waterfalls and ocean waves, so that next time it rains, you can walk out and feel the touch of angels' wings.

# THE
# WATERS
# ABOVE

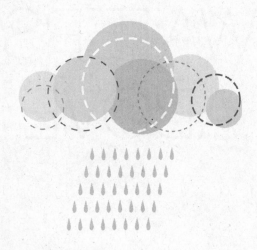

# The Gift of Rain

Setting aside all tiredness,
I rain down the rain of the Dharma.
When I rain down the rain of the Dharma,
Then all this world is well refreshed.

Saddharmapundarika Sutra

When I was ten, drought took hold of the region where my family had a cattle property. The creek shrank into a series of stagnant waterholes, the swamps and lagoons dried up altogether and the water birds that nested in the reeds flew away. The drought persisted for three years. During that time calves and foals were born that had come to maturity without ever having seen rain.

Then, one hot summer day it rained . . . and rained . . . and rained, the rain increasing in intensity so that for a while it was difficult to see far beyond the fence that surrounded our house. We all gathered on the wide front verandah watching the rain sheeting down, hearing the loud insistent rhythm drumming on the galvanised iron roof, breathing in the fresh cool ionised air.

Suddenly, as the downfall diminished in intensity, the curtain of water lifted to reveal a scene that remains indelibly imprinted on my memory.

Our Herefords were dancing in the rain!

A rain dance performed by 200 cattle, their red hides and white heads glistening and wet, is a sight to behold. The movements are slow and rhythmic, simple but defined. Jump up on the back feet with the front feet lifted about a metre, then down onto the front feet and lift the back legs with a slight kick. And then begin again. The horses galloped wildly among the groups of dancing cattle, whinnying and shaking water off their manes and tails.

It was such a magnificent spectacle that part of me wanted to throw off my clothes and join in their celebration, but of course, I didn't. I was only ten.

I would now. Now I understand.

The rain dance is primeval, a spontaneous physical response. The waters inside us rejoicing at seeing the water above reunited with the water below. The tingling primal exuberance of dancing naked in the rain after a long dry is something all of us should experience at least once in our lives—animals or humans, it doesn't matter.

It was the desire to reproduce this sensation of divine communion that led Sergius Orata, a Roman entrepreneur, to invent the first shower or 'rain bath' in 95 BC 'where seas of hot water were confined aloft'. Thus the miracle of the rain was integrated into the bathhouses of those who could afford to indulge themselves in such sensual luxuries.

The body's response to rain, however artificial, remains spontaneous.

Although the sterile shower stall of the twenty-first century is far too confined to perform a proper rain dance, many still feel inspired to sing, singing naked in the virtual rain, just like our ancestors. Vestiges of ancient rain chants and dances persist in popular culture. Who could forget the contagious enthusiasm of Gene Kelly singing in the rain while tap dancing in soggy pumps? It's a great Hollywood salute to a traditional celebration that's thousands of years old.

This strange, magical substance we call rain, where does it come from? Opinions vary. No matter who you ask, no matter where they live or what they believe, everyone has an answer. Religious folk, and I include myself, assert that their particular god or gods, or a Supreme Being, is responsible. Scientists, on the other hand, tell us that no-one makes the rain, that it's simply part of the 'water cycle'. Water evaporates, forms clouds, comes down as rain. End of story. But that perspective of the water cycle as a mechanical process devoid of spirit and empty of meaning is just one version of an ancient tale that began with the first human looking up into the storm clouds and wondering, 'Who is doing this?'.

Two thousand five hundred years ago the Taoist philosopher Chaung Tzu wrote:

> Clouds cause rain,
> Rain causes clouds,
> Wind comes from the north.
> Now it blows east, now west.
> And now it whirls aloft.
> Who puffs it forth?

Who has the leisure to be doing all this?
I should like to know.

So who makes the rain? Is it an act of God or nature?

Among the folktales of Braj in India is a story which tells of a time when Indra was worshipped as the God of rain. Krishna, a divinity incarnated as a mortal, just as Jesus was, called the people together to tell them that their prayers and offerings to Indra were a waste of time. Instead Krishna taught the people to worship nature, to direct their devotion to streams, forests, rocks and mountains, especially Mount Govardhan in the centre of Braj. When the people brought the mountain gifts of fruit and flowers and sweetmeats, Krishna transformed himself into a mountain God who received the offerings and consumed them. Happy to see their gifts accepted by the deity, the people went away singing the praises of nature.

Indra was enraged.

He vowed to sweep the blasphemers from the face of the Earth. Indra commanded the King of Clouds to rain over Braj and Mount Govardhan until both were washed away. An army of black clouds surrounded Braj, pouring down rain so fiercely that the people, in fear of their lives, turned to Krishna for help. 'You persuaded us to give up the worship of Indra. Now protect us from his wrath,' they begged.

Krishna obliged. Infusing Mount Govardhan with

the heat of his energy, he turned it upside down, balancing it on the point of his finger so that it became a huge glowing umbrella. Under this shelter the people and the cows of Braj gathered in safety. As the rain fell on the white hot mountain it hissed and evaporated into clouds of steam so that not one drop fell on Braj.

Defeated, Indra came down from Heaven, knelt at Krishna's feet and submitted to him. Krishna played his flute, the sun shone, streams sparkled with light and from that time on the people of Braj have worshipped nature as the source of rain.

Many Christians, Hindus, Muslims and Jews, and countless indigenous cultures, believe that rain is sent by a capricious sky deity who looks down from his, or her, home in the clouds and sends the rain when he, or she, is so inclined. Historically, the function of rain-makers, be they priests, lamas, shamans, witchdoctors or rabbis, was to intercede with the appropriate deity and, if necessary, persuade (or sometimes even compel) the Spirit-in-the-Sky to release the essential life-giving rain.

If the supplications of the drought-stricken received no response, the gods were sometimes blamed and shamed.

In the Middle Ages, images of Christian saints were punished for not answering people's prayers for rain. In some areas the practice continued into the nineteenth century. In 1893 there was a severe drought on the island of Sicily. After six months of fruitless prayer the infuriated peasants threw the statues of local saints into horse ponds, tore off their embroidered robes and pushed them face down into the parched gardens so that they could see for themselves how serious the situation was. When rain eventually fell, the peasants reverently returned the saints back to their respective niches.

Conversely, there's a story about a saint who stopped the rain and a courtesan who made it fall again. In Buddhist circles it's known as the tale of the One-horned Rishi. Ekasringa, the *rishi* (saint) with one horn, was the son of a remote forest-dwelling ascetic and a doe, a female deer. Little is said about Ekasringa's mother who left home for greener pastures not long after the birth.

Born in the wilderness and brought up by his father, Ekasringa knew nothing of the world except the spartan hermitage he called home. He had never seen another person and was unaware of the existence of women. His father died when he was eighteen and from that time on Ekasringa devoted himself to the study of magic. He spent weeks in ecstatic trance communing with spirits from whom he acquired supernatural powers.

One day while the young hermit was descending the steep mountain track, heavy rain fell making the path slippery and muddy. In his trance state Ekasringa did not notice until he slipped and broke his ankle. He was so angry he used a magic spell to stop the rain. Soon a great drought spread over the entire land, crops failed and the people cried out for food.

The King of Benares called his wise men together and asked them how to end the drought. They could think of only one solution. If the sage Ekasringa could be reduced to the condition of an ordinary man, they said, his supernatural powers would cease and his magic formula would lose its effect. To this end the King sent for Kamala, a courtesan skilled in the art of love, and explained the situation. Not only would she seduce the young mystic, said Kamala, she would return to Benares carried on his shoulders.

Gathering a retinue of beautiful courtesans, Kamala set off for the forest. On her head each woman carried a basket of gifts of cakes, sweetmeats and wine. When they arrived at One-horn's retreat, the women presented themselves as anchorites, devotees anxious for instruction. Leaving their clothes hidden in the forest, the women had fashioned skimpy costumes of leaves and bark such as might appeal to a forest ascetic.

For an innocent young man who had never seen a woman before, Ekasringa behaved with restraint and courtesy. Inviting them to sit he accepted the gifts of wine, which they told him was a special water, and the sweet cakes which they said were fruit. When he had drunk and eaten his fill of wine and delicacies, Ekasringa sat back in a daze. The taste of sugar was new to him. 'Since I was born,' he said, 'I have never seen fruit or water like these. How did you come by them?'

'We practise good with all our heart,' replied Kamala demurely fluttering her long lashes. 'That is why Heaven grants our desires and gives us this fruit and this water.'

'Stay here with me,' said the young man, 'and we will share these delights.' That night the inevitable happened. Ekasringa lost his virginity and his magic power, and heavy rain fell.

When the gifts had been consumed, the rishi found the taste of forest fruit and mountain water so insipid he agreed to accompany his female entourage to the place where these luxuries originated. As they came within sight of Benares, Kamala said she was tired and could go no further. 'Climb up on my shoulders,' said her obliging young lover. And, just as she had said, Kamala entered riding on the rishi.

'Before you can make rain it is important to know if something is preventing the rain from falling,' said a Chinese sage.

In one of his lectures, Carl Jung told of a Taoist rain-maker who was sent for by the mayor of a drought-stricken Chinese village. He arrived carrying a small bag and asked only that an empty hut be made available to him and his meals delivered to the door so that he did not have to leave. After a week rain fell. When the rainmaker emerged from the hut, the mayor asked him what he had done. Was it magic, he wanted to know?

'Not at all,' replied the rainmaker. 'What I did with my meditation was to bring the disparate energies of the place into a harmonic convergence. Once that was achieved rain could fall once more.'

Rainmaking is one of the most noble and mysterious of the magic arts. *The Annals of Rome* chronicle an intriguing episode that occurred during the wars of the Emperor Marcus Aurelius in which Harnouphis, Heirogrammat of Egypt, conjured up a miraculous rainstorm which saved the Roman army from defeat.

More recently, in the summer of 1923 when China was in the grip of a severe drought, the Tashi Lama, living in exile in Bejing, offered to perform a prayer for rain. Ten thousand people came to witness the ceremony. At 10 am incense was lit, the Lama drew a circle on the ground and recited this short prayer: 'Lord of the World, I swear by thy great name that I will not move from this place where I kneel until you take pity on your children and send rain.' Hours passed. Some of the crowd went home. However, at 4 pm clouds began to build and a two-hour deluge followed.

Can human beings communicate with clouds and winds? The answer appears to be yes, but the tools of trade and the processes rainmakers employ to call down rain differ from culture to culture. These ceremonies have rarely been documented in detail by Western observers. Secrecy is an essential element in the shaman's mystique; it is necessary to prevent the ritual being performed by the uninitiated.

*The Rainmaker*, a recent biography of Lama Yeshi Dorje, contains descriptions of Tibetan weather-controlling ceremonies. Although Yeshi Dorje comes from a famous family of rainmakers, indicating that his gifts may be hereditary, it took years of training and meditation before he could manifest them.

Photographs of one rainmaking rite show the Lama surrounded by smoking fires, blowing a trumpet made out of a human thighbone while pointing at the clouds with his *Dorje* (thunderbolt) dagger. Gradually clouds began to form, becoming larger and darker until within hours rain and hail fell. On that occasion, at the request of the local farmers, he kept it raining for a week. Yeshi Dorje Rinpoche spent the next forty years as a rainmaker in Tibet and later in India where his skills made him a legend.

In 1975, the Australian anthropologist Charles Mountford recorded and photographed a group of Pitjatjanjara rainmakers during a three-day ceremony which was followed by heavy rain. Mountford was astonished. The Simpson Desert had been in drought for five years and yet these men had been able to make rain to expedite the expedition's journey. Baffled, Mountford wrote in his journal: 'There does not seem to be a logical explanation for the success of this ceremony.'

To the Bushmen of the Kalahari Desert the rain is a large animal which lives in a deep secluded pool. Wherever it walks on the land, rain will fall. The rain-doctor's job is to lasso the animal with a leather rope and drag or lead it over the land in his dreams. Then the clouds will come. The dark cumulo-nimbus rain clouds are the visible manifestation of the giant beast; its legs the columns of descending rain. Quiet, gentle rain is female, a Rain-cow. A heavy deluge with much thunder and lightning indicates the activity of the bellowing Rain-bull.

Not everyone is intimidated by thunder and lightning. North American Indian people invoke the dark power of the Thunderbird and the male rain that accompanies it. The Night Chant, a traditional nine-day Navaho ceremony climaxes in a rainmaking ritual performed by a circle of shamans wearing the masks of the Gods.

'With your mind enveloped in dark cloud,
come to us,' they sing,

'With the near darkness made of the dark cloud of the rain and the mist, come to us,

With the darkness on the earth, come to us.'

This emphasis on the darkness of rain clouds reminds us that black is the symbolic colour of rain, which is why Zulu rainmakers burn the area around which they perform their rituals. Smoking fires are another common ingredient. Heavy black smoke is often associated with rain.

When threatened by drought, farmers in the north of England piled masses of wild fern into huge black smoking bonfires to remind the Celt rain deities that it was time to shower down their blessings. This activity must have been reasonably effective because when King Charles I was travelling through the English county of Staffordshire in 1636, he ordered that no fern be burned until he left because 'the burning of Ferne doth draw downe rain'.

Fire plays a prominent part in Chinese and Japanese rainmaking. In the theory of the Five Elements, any event may be explained as the product of the interplay between the principles exemplified by wood, earth, fire, metal and water. In the order of destructive potentiality, fire destroys wood, water quenches fire. So a large ceremonial fire or a procession of flaming torches accompanied by prayers for rain and the chanting of incantations, call down water from the sky to restore the natural harmony. Australian desert aborigines burn spinifex grass which grows in round clumps resembling young clouds; North American Indian peoples and Tibetans use specific woods and grasses to help produce the desired effect.

There are alternatives to elaborate magic ceremonies. In some parts of the world it seems that all you have to do is shout!

At the foot of the Gaoligan Mountains in Yunnan, China, is The Mysterious Lake, which appears to respond to the human voice. Whenever anyone speaks loudly beside the lake, heavy rain follows; the louder the speaker and the longer they speak the longer the rain lasts. A story in the *Shanghai Liberation Daily*, (24 February 1981), describes how an aggressive Communist Party official went and shouted at the lake, 'whereupon in less than a minute it began to rain'. The explanation offered was that because the air is so moist, the slightest vibration can cause it to precipitate.

'Clouds follow the dragon,' says Confucius in his commentary on the hexagram *K'ien* in the *I Ching*. Its six identical horizontal lines, one above the other, symbolically depict the Chinese water cycle as six manifestations of the dragon, from 'Hidden Dragon', through 'Swooping', 'Flying', 'Visible', 'Leaping', until finally it descends 'In the fields' as rain. Thunderstorms are dragons fighting in the sky and rain is the consequence of their conflict. From this vision, ways of relating to the mythical beasts embedded themselves deeply in Chinese culture.

The original function of the annual Hong Kong dragon boat race was to remind the dragons that it was time to battle one another again and bring on the rains of spring. Dragon dances and processions performed in every Chinese community by groups of people carrying long dragon costumes, accompanied by drums, gongs and firecrackers, began as ceremonies designed to wake the sleeping dragon who was withholding the rain.

The Giant Snake Ancestor in the guise of dragons, lizards and snakes appears in rites and practices performed by indigenous people throughout the world who believe that reptiles have the power to confine and control the rain. Snake charmers are often hereditary rainmakers.

In his *Theogeny*, Hesiod envisages the ocean as a great python with its nine protective coils encircling the Earth. Egyptian hieroglyphs depict the Nile God hiding in a coiled serpent, while Aztec scrolls show the Rain God Tláoc and his adversary, the Water Confining Snake, side by side. In southeast Asia dragon snake divinities, known as Nagas, are the Masters of Rain.

The Rainbow Serpent of central Australia, a giant python whose scales gleam with colour, regulates the waters above and below, and the clouds in the sky. He speaks with the voice of thunder, his lovemaking, lightning and rain. When he sleeps, drought appears. The Rainbow Serpent leaves rain-stones as evidence of his passing. These small white quartz crystals are infused with the spirits of the ancestors. The most potent magic water is envisaged as liquid quartz. One desert traveller observed that: 'None of the medicine-man's possessions is more revered than quartz crystals. They are used for rainmaking and are held to possess marvellous powers.'

The custodians of Uluru tend the sacred pool at the base of the rock that is the home of the Rainbow Snake. Visitors are warned not to profane it in any way lest they anger the spirit and cause the surrounding springs to dry up.

Vritra, the drought demon of India, is another serpent dragon that confines the waters. In the Vedic hymns, Indra the Lord of Water, slays Vritra and releases the rain to fall once more.

'God is falling,' Bantu people sing, celebrating the first rains of the season.

'As it comes from above, so rain links humans with the divine. Rain is a deeply religious rhythm and those who deal in it transact business of the highest religious calibre,' writes John Mbiti in *African Religion and Philosophy*. 'Rain is the manifestation of the eternal in the here and now. Rainmakers not only seek physical rain but symbolise man's contact with the blessings of time and eternity.' Hindu scriptures describe 'subtle' beings that descend from the moon to earth dissolved in rain drops, which in turn connects with the esoteric Islamic belief that: 'With every drop of rain God sends his angel.'

In the remote northern Kimberley region of Western Australia, cloud people known as *Wandjina* are the ancestors who generate the life spirits of the Aboriginal people living there. Originating from *wandjina* in the clouds, these spirits fall as rain and live in the water that results. When a woman drinks, the life spirit enters her and, through her, her yet-to-be-born child. Life spirits also inhabit fish, crayfish, turtles and other creatures born in water.

One elder put it this way: 'Our fathers may have found us in the form of fish or turtles, but the *wandjina* is our real father. It was he who put us in the water from the sky . . . that's how we came down from heaven, through water, by dreams.' Paintings of *wandjina* in the caves of the Kimberleys show some as clouds. Their eyes are dark circles while the outer edges of the cloud form the characteristic halo from which lightning radiates. Surrounding dot patterns signify the rain-bearing life spirits.

If each raindrop is a vehicle in which spirits make the journey between Heaven and Earth, how do we welcome them? How do we celebrate their arrival and ensure continuity? How do we express our gratitude?

Think before you drink, and give thanks to the giver.

Traditional Tibetan medicine recommends rain water because it's vitalising, refreshing, pleasing to the stomach, thin, satisfying, stimulating to the intellect, of indistinct taste, savoury, light, cool, and nectar-like, touched by the sun, moon and wind.

Collect your own in an earthenware (rather than glass) bowl next time it rains. And while you're drinking remember that all rain is the Rain of the Dharma.

# Cloudland—
# Home of the Immortals

In the immense void of the sky, clouds arise.
They come from nowhere and they go nowhere.
Nowhere exists a storehouse of clouds. They arise
in the empty spaces of heaven and dissolve
therein, like thoughts in the human mind.

The Buddha

The movement and formation of clouds offers us the spectacle of water at play, dancing daily before the azure curtain of the sky. How many of us take the time to honour this miracle, to stand in reverence before it?

More than you might imagine.

At the base of Mount Yufu on the Japanese island of Kushu is the hot-spring town of Yufuin, made famous by the many writers who have gone there for peace, tranquillity and inspiration. I had come briefly to sample the waters while on a pilgrimage around the hot springs of Japan in 1994. Yufuin is built around Lake Kinrin whose reedy shore is surrounded by pine trees. On my first morning there I was up early to photograph the floating mists that rose off the lake, concealing then revealing groves of pines and an antique thatch-roofed bathhouse on the shore.

I had set up my tripod and taken a good many images when, out of the mist, a woman appeared. Apologising for her halting English, she said that she and her family had been watching me from their hotel. They wondered if I would like to come with them to see something wonderful, to watch the sun rise over the Sea of Clouds.

I accepted immediately without further question, and joined them in their large black Mercedes. The road wound up through the misty pine forests of Mount Yufu. As we rose higher the mists dispersed. Ten minutes later we arrived at a parking area and lookout bustling with activity in the pre-dawn light. Tourist buses disgorged passengers, cars parked; some people were setting up cameras and tripods while others crowded around the edge of the stone parapet.

There, stretched out below, was the deep round valley of Yufuin, transformed into a vast natural basin filled with mist and cloud. As the first rays of the rising sun spread across the Sea of Clouds, its level surface became suffused with a burnished red-gold that, as we watched, slowly faded to a rosy pink. Everyone was still, silent with the wonder of it. The dawn chorus of the forest birds echoed around us. It was a vision of such rare beauty that it remains indelibly imprinted on my memory.

Some white-clad devotees of Shinto prayed to the *Kami*, the spirit deities that inhabit the clouds, the valleys and the mountains, in whose presence we stood spellbound. I, too, gave thanks to the *Kami* for arranging this mythic journey to the Sea of Clouds without any effort on my part.

It seems to be agreed among the religions of the world that clouds are the abode of the gods. The cloud-masked rain-bringers of the North American Zuni, the god of the Old Testament and the Koran, the deities of ancient Greece and Rome, and the Maruts of the

*Rig Veda*, are just a few of the residents of Cloudland. There are so many deities that the Navaho gave them a generic name; they call them the Cloud People.

Sometimes Cloud People approach humans directly, but there are few firsthand records of such encounters. One rare meeting with a Cloud Person was recorded by Alexandra David-Neel. David-Neel was an extraordinary writer, explorer and spiritual adventurer who spent 14 years in Tibet from 1915 to 1929. A no-nonsense sceptic, she was a practising Buddhist who was so highly regarded by the Tibetan religious hierarchy that they made her an honorary Lama.

In *Magic and Mystery in Tibet*, David-Neel tells of a night when she camped alone beside a clear lake in a barren and inhospitable wilderness. Then, 'As evening darkened the bright mirror of the lake the fantastic procession of clouds lighted by the moon marched along the neighbouring summits and descended towards the valleys surrounding me with a troop of nebulous phantoms. One of them came forward walking alone over a path of light, suddenly spread out on the dark water, like a carpet before his steps.

'The transparent giant, whose eyes were two stars, made a gesture with his long arm emerging from a floating robe. Did he call me? Did he drive me away? . . . I could not tell.

'Then he approached still nearer, looking so real, so

life-like, that I closed my eyes to dispel the hallucination. I felt myself wrapped in the folds of a soft cold cloak whose subtle substance penetrated me, causing me to shiver . . .'

Another description of Cloud People appears in a seventeenth-century London pamphlet under the heading 'Strange News from the West'. It tells how 'divers persons of credit', who happened to be crossing London Bridge at 8 pm March 21, 1661, witnessed the astonishing spectacle of 'two great armies marching forth of two clouds, and encountering each other, but after a sharp dispute they suddenly vanished'. Then emerging from another cloud 'that seemed like a mountain' came a procession of animals 'in the shapes of a bull, a bear, a lion and an elephant with a castle on his back'.

Cloud People are shape shifters extraordinaire, transforming themselves into symbolic landscapes of meaning, inhabited by animals, humans and powerful monsters whose thunder shakes the ground as their lightning illuminates the darkness. Since the beginning of time, Cloud People have provided endless visual entertainment, spiritual instruction, inspiration and, of course, sustenance in the form of rain and snow. For the hunter-gatherers it was the equivalent of widescreen daytime television permanently tuned to Sky Channel. For those of us who stubbornly remain disconnected from TV, the Cloud People are still the most consistently entertaining show in town.

Hidden behind their cloud masks, the Uwanami, the industrious rain bringers of the Zuni Indians, fill their gourds at the springs of the six great waters of the cosmic world. Also known as the Shadow People, the Uwanami are the spirits of deceased Zuni men and women. They pour their precious water through the clouds, each cloud acting as a sieve that distributes the water evenly.

Among the most beautiful and popular of the Cloud People are the heavenly dancers, the Apsaras, whose name in Sanskrit means essence of water (*Ap*, 'water' and *sara*, 'essence'). The Apsaras can take any form they choose, but their favourite incarnations are beautiful women or clouds.

In November 1997, American Mike Valeri, took a photo of a cloud formation in which a white angelic figure can be seen floating above a full moon. His cloudscape image sold to newspapers all over the world. Cynics said it was either a lucky accident or a careful photoshop adjustment. To me, she looked just like one of the smiling Apsaras carved in stone on the pillars of the temples of Ankor Wat.

Since clouds are associated with the fertility brought by rain, it's not surprising that they are imagined by some to have a sexual nature. The Hindi cloud goddess Rati (lust), for instance, was the energetic wife of Kama, the god of erotic desire. She is said to have enjoyed making love with any god, mortal, beast, river, plant or tree that took her fancy.

Frigg, the dignified Norse goddess of clouds, sister of Thor the thunder god and wife of Odin, wore snow-white, grey or dark cloud ensembles according to her mood. She lived an independent existence with her handmaidens in Fensalir, the Hall of Mists where they spun and wove clouds with Frigg's jewelled distaff.

In a Roman myth, Jupiter (the Roman version of The Greek Zeus) conceals himself within a dark cloud in order to make love to the exquisite Io, the mortal priestess of his wife, Juno. Io tried to run away through the forest, writes the Roman poet Ovid, 'but the god called forth a heavy shadow which involved the wide extended earth, and stopped her flight and ravished in that cloud her chastity'.

In China, it is the ubiquitous dragons whose breath becomes the clouds in which they conceal themselves. On the mortal plane, the act of sexual union is sometimes referred to as the 'cloud and rain game'—clouds representing the blending of the polarities of male and female, yang and yin. Rain is the fluid climax of their bonding. 'Fragrant clouds' is an enchanting Chinese metaphor for beautiful hair floating free, while an enticingly full décolletage is *Yun-Wu*, 'cloud fog'.

The symbolism of cloud forms and their interpretation dates from the day our ancestors first looked for meaning and significance in the phenomena of nature. The sky was an obvious place to start. Thus began the endless and continuing debate about whether the clouds carry messages or not.

The Romans, and the Greeks before them, placed great importance on cloud interpretation. One famous cloud reader was the philosopher Appolonius. In one of his dialogues, Appolonius broached the possibility that God creates and colours each cloud form.

I wish someone had told me that when I was ten.

Before the advent of Playstation, Gameboy and the internet, cloud watching was a popular childhood pastime. We'd lie on our backs for hours as image after image unfolded across the sky; dragons followed armies of knights on horseback charging one another with their swords and lances before morphing into dignified processions of silent figures floating off to their home beyond the sunset.

I didn't know then that there were Buddhist monks whose daily devotional ritual consists of lying on mountaintops meditating on the movement, nature and forms of clouds. It's a religion I would have embraced more enthusiastically than the sombre masses of the High Church of England where I carried the cross on Sundays.

But we learned a lot about clouds in church too.

We learned from the Old Testament how God had transformed himself into a pillar of cloud to lead the children of Israel on their long journey out of Egypt, across the Red Sea and through the desert to their final destination. The cloud told Moses and his followers when to move and when to stop.

The activities of clouds feature prominently in the New Testament as well. Matthew describes how Jesus took three disciples for a retreat up on a high mountaintop. Jesus becomes transfigured, clothed in white light, Moses and Elijah appear, and then God descends in the form of a supportive talking cloud. And later in Matthew, when Jesus is interrogated by the authorities as to his true identity, he replies: 'Hereafter shall ye see the son of man sitting on the right hand of power and coming in the clouds of heaven.'

One of the most famous symbols of Christendom first appeared as a cloud formation. On 27 October AD 312, the army of the Byzantine Emperor Constantine was enroute to Rome to do battle with the Emperor Augustus for the Eastern Empire. Suddenly, as the army and its leader watched, the clouds above began to shape themselves into a large X with a letter P running through its centre. This is the *Chi Rho*, the monogram of Christ in Greek, being the first two letters of the holy name—X, meaning *Chi* and P, meaning *Rho*.

That night in his tent, Constantine had a dream in which Christ told him to make a likeness of the sign he had seen in the heavens and to use it in all engagements with his enemies. Accordingly, Constantine ordered battle standards to be made bearing the divine insignia, later called the *Labarum* of Constantine. It was a great success. Although they were outnumbered, Constantine's army triumphed under their new banner and as a direct consequence of this victory, Christianity eventually became the dominant religion of the Roman Empire.

Clouds also helped to identify the fourteenth Dalai Lama. Not long after the passing of the 'Great Thirteenth' in December 1933, a cluster of unusual clouds in the shape of dragons and elephants illuminated by spectacular rainbows gathered over the city of Lhasa. The oracles interpreted this as a sign that an event of great spiritual significance had taken place, perhaps even the birth of the next Dalai Lama.

Two years later, the Regent and a party of lamas set off to search for the reincarnated leader of their faith. They gathered on the shores of Lake Namtso, the home of a powerful protective deity. It is claimed that on the surface of its waters initiates see visions of the future in the reflected images of the clouds above. The waiting monks saw a monastery roofed with copper and gold beside a winding road that led to a nearby mountain shaped like an elephant. Where the road met the mountain, there was a small house with distinctive carved gables painted blue, and, under a blooming peach tree, was a woman holding a baby. This, they knew to be the fourteenth Dalai Lama. The vision was recorded and sealed so that it could not be tampered with. When the Dalai Lama was finally discovered, it was as the clouds had foretold.

Buddhist scriptures utilise clouds as a metaphor to communicate the idea that illusion and reality are interchangeable mental constructs. According to the first-century *Prajna Paramita*, the forms that we think of as everyday reality are fleeting, insubstantial and transient; the true nature of reality resembles the shape changing of clouds and dream images.

*The Book of Clouds* and other Tibetan texts provide guidance for novices wishing to attain enlightenment by meditating on the movement and formation of clouds. As always, the teachings of the Buddha are a continuing source of inspiration and lucidity.

Prolonged contemplation of the sky leads to a peculiar trance in which the notion of personality is replaced by an indescribable feeling of union with the universe. The sky is a mirror in which we can redis-cover the true extent of the knowledge and wisdom that lies concealed within. Just as a mirror will show you an image of your face, so when you turn your gaze upward to the vault of heaven you can see there the reflection of your mind's eye.

Here is a simple exercise in sky and cloud meditation. Find a place with an uninterrupted view of the sky. Seashores, beaches, deserts, mountaintops, lookouts or the rooftops of high apartment buildings are ideal. Make yourself comfortable in a horizontal position. Clearing the mind of all extraneous thought and distraction, direct your attention to a point in the sky and keep it fixed on this point. Consider the Buddha's teaching on the nature of clouds at the beginning of this chapter. Let the sky reflect your mind. Let the infinitude of the blue void be an empty screen on which your thoughts appear. Do not attach any importance to any form that the clouds may take. Do not look for any meaning. Be content just to be.

Eventually and inevitably as clouds form, images appear.

Initially, you may think that these visions are external; but with time and continuing daily concentration you will come to recognise that what you are seeing up there is a projection of your mind, which is itself an extension of the Divine Mind. The practice will have served its purpose when it has demonstrated that the entire universe, above and below, is a continuous creation of your own mind.

Here's another thought. If the clouds in the sky are an extension of your conscious or unconscious mind, will they respond to your command?

In *Illusions—The Diary of a Reluctant Messiah*, Richard Bach includes a discussion of the practice of telepathic cloud vaporisation—dispersing a cloud by concentrating the mind on it. Cloud summoning and cloud busting have always been among the powers possessed by shamans and magicians. Such demonstrations were performed in ancient China and continue to be recorded in indigenous communities.

Clouds contain mysteries that defy rational explanation, mysteries dismissed as phenomena by scientists and meteorologists for whom clouds are just masses of water vapour with Latin names.

The demystification of clouds began in 1803 when Luke Howard, an amateur naturalist in England, proposed a system of names and categories by which clouds could easily be identified. Howard divided cloud formations into three basic categories. The most common white fluffy cauliflower-shaped clouds he called *cumulus* ('heap' or 'pile' in Latin); *stratus* meaning 'layer' for those thick grey blankets that cover the sky and blot out the sun; and *cirrus* ('cord' or 'tuft') for the delicate silken drifting filaments. Howard qualified each of these generic names with more specific designations; *nimbus*, being Latin for rain and *alto*, meaning high. This small vocabulary has gradually expanded to describe the structure and activity of 26 cloud types.

But does it? Does it really? Can such terms adequately communicate wonder and beauty and endless variety? These are subjective values beyond the possibility of scientific explanation. 'I, standing twenty miles off, see a crimson cloud on the horizon' writes Henry Thoreau. 'You tell me it is a mass of vapour which absorbs all other rays and reflects the red, but that is nothing to the purpose, for this red vision excites me, stirs my blood, makes my thoughts flow . . . What sort of science is that which enriches the understanding, but robs the imagination?'

The astronomer Sir Fred Hoyle, a prolific writer and science communicator, bridged this gap between science and imagination in *The Black Cloud*, a work of science fiction in which an intelligent cloud is the central character. Black clouds bring the heavy black rain of destruction and are often associated with depression. In 'I feel a dark cloud hanging over me', black clouds present a menacing and intimidating aspect. The apocalyptic vision of St Thomas Aquinas begins: 'Beholding from afar off I saw a great cloud looming black over the whole earth . . .'

This was the inspiration for Hoyle's tale of a massive black cloud that originates in the constellation of Orion and settles on the sun in order to absorb its energy, causing the Earth to heat dramatically. There is extensive destruction and loss of life followed by a month of darkness during which the black cloud initiates contact with humans. Unfortunately, the intelligence of the cloud far surpasses that of the scientists who are communicating with it. In vain the black cloud tries to convey its knowledge and wisdom to American and British astronomers, but it is too much for them and two die from cosmic intellectual overload. Bored, the cloud finally moves on and the sun shines once more.

*The Black Cloud* has a message for us too. It reminds us that the Divine Intelligence that permeates the universe is beyond our understanding, beyond even our capacity to understand. The only appropriate response is awe, humility, reverence and love.

Maybe then we'll be in the right state of mind to hear what it is the Cloud People are trying to tell us.

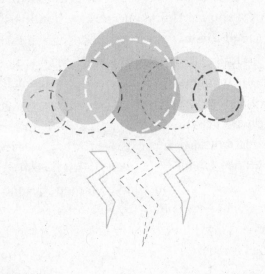

# Thunder—
# The Voice of Baiame

Then I saw another mighty angel…robed in a
cloud, with a rainbow above his head…when he
shouted, the voices of the seven thunders spoke.
And when the seven thunders spoke, I was about
to write; but I heard a voice from heaven say,
'Seal up what the seven thunders have said and
do not write it down.'

The Book of Revelation

I've often wondered what secrets the seven thunders told John in his vision. Did the thunders speak in human voices or in the ominous rumblings with which we are all familiar?

Baiame, creator of indigenous Australians, speaks with the voice of thunder through his instrument, the bull-roarer. The bronze thunder drums of China and Japan, the slit-log drums of New Guinea and the Pacific Islands, and indeed the earliest examples of the drum itself, all were created in imitation of the voice of thunder.

But who could speak its language? Who could interpret its meaning?

Centuries before John had his revelatory vision, a prophet in Tuscany was entrusted with the secrets of 'the voices of the thunders'. And she did write them down. These sacred texts on thunder and lightning divination, known as the *Books of Begoia*, 'were renowned throughout the ancient world' according to the Greek historian, Diodorus. Just as the Chinese *Book of Clouds* assisted initiates to read the messages of water written in the sky, so did the *Books of Begoia* allow the Etruscan priests to interpret the language of water as heard in the thunder and seen in the lightning flash. The books contained the visions and revelations of Begoia, a sibyl whose teachings included mathematics and the geometric proportions and rules for dividing land and surveying boundaries.

Eturia, the home of the Etruscans, because of its volcanic nature and its geology, attracts more violent and frequent thunderstorms than elsewhere. So it's not surprising that the Etruscans were the first to develop a methodology for the interpretation of thunder and lightning, including directions for expiation if the omens were unfavourable. The sky was sub-divided into sixteen regions and distinctions made between the colours of lightning, its shape and the direction from which it flashed. Lightning in the east was thought to be particularly auspicious.

Another of Begoia's books dealt exclusively with the *Fuluratura*, the art of summoning and controlling lightning. Pliny tells a story of a monster named Volta which devastated a city in Eturia and how the Etruscan augurs generated lightning to kill it. Although this was an unlikely event, belief in the Etruscans' ability to do such things earned them great respect. As late as 408 AD Etruscan priests were supposed to have called down lightning on the invading hordes of the Visigoth king Alaric.

The shamans of northern Siberia, too, invoked lightning and thunder in the form of a giant black bird with claws of iron. Thunderbirds constitute an entire species of supernatural beings. Priests of ancient Babylon directed their prayers to Imdugud, the great black bird whose storm clouds covered the sky, consuming the Bull of Heaven before his hot breath could scorch the crops below.

The North American thunderbird accompanied the Siberian tribes on their migration to the east to become one of the chief sky gods of the Indian people of Canada and the United States. Their thunderbirds wear cloaks of eagle feathers. When their wings flap thunder sounds and lightning flashes as they open and close their eyes. Anything struck by this lightning whether it be tree, rock, animal or human is infused with spiritual power. Thunderbirds are engaged in an ongoing battle with the serpents of the underworld, causing violent floods, earthquakes and thunder-storms.

Thunder and lightning are manifestations of water's awesome power against which none can stand. The heat generated by a single lightning flash is intense beyond imagining. Within millionths of a second it may reach 50,000°F, five times the temperature of the surface of the sun. And it has been estimated that lightning strikes the Earth around 100 times every second, generating a massive four billion kilowatts of electric power.

The action of lightning and its generation remain a mystery. While lightning may be defined as 'the visible electric emission from a charged cloud', it is not known how the cloud became electrified in the first place. It is thought that when the temperature of a cloud reaches freezing point, droplets of negatively charged water attract positively charged ice particles. The updraft/downdraft movement of air within the cloud separates out the water which descends, while the lighter ice crystals rise. Immense electrical stresses build up between these two polarities capable of generating as much as 100 million volts. When a sufficiently high charge has accumulated, it overcomes the electrical resistance of the air and a lightning flash occurs. This may happen entirely within a cloud or along horizontal planes between clouds.

Thunder is the sound produced by the rapid expansion and contraction of gases within the channel of the lightning flash. By timing the interval between lightning and thunder it's possible to make a reasonably accurate estimate of the distance between you and an oncoming storm. Allow six seconds for every mile or kilometre.

It is said that lightning never strikes the same place twice, but this is not true. The Empire State Building and the Eiffel Tower are struck on average twenty or thirty times a year, because of their extreme height. Before Benjamin Franklin's invention of the lightning conductor, this was the fate of many tall buildings—church steeples, lighthouses, castles and palaces—all could be brought down in seconds.

To prehistoric people it seemed as if lightning was a massive stone axe that fell from the sky without warning, wielded by an angry deity whose rumbling rage shook the mountains and echoed through the valleys. It left a trail of shattered rocks, splintered trees and maimed or dead humans and animals as if a giant madman had run amok with a primitive stone-age tool. How could one placate such a powerful force? What could be offered as a sacrifice to appease its anger?

The customs and traditions of the Semang pygmies, a Kensiu tribe on the Malay peninsula, preserved from long ago, give us an insight into the response of Paleolithic humans to lightning and the thunder that accompanies it. The Semang believe that a god named Pedn creates thunder, throwing down lightning bolts because he is offended by the breaking of taboos and other transgressions. The only thing that will pacify him is human blood.

A woman begins the ritual, rhythmically beating her calf with the handle of a spoon made out of coconut shell. Others chant in a circle around her. Piercing the spot with the point of a sharp sacrificial blade, she drives the knife in further, striking it with repeated blows of the spoon handle until the blood runs freely. She scrapes the wound with the blade, catching the blood and transferring it to a bamboo container carved with lightning symbols where it is mixed with water. Some of the mixture is poured back into the spoon and thrown into the sky by the shaman. The ceremony is repeated until the sacrifice is accepted and the storm subsides. This is a vestige of more bloody ancient rituals best left unremembered.

Experts on the subject tell us that, probably because of their geology or hydrology, some areas attract more storms than others. The city of Bogor in Java holds the world record—322 days of thunder in a year. Tampa, Florida has the highest average in the United States at 94. These places are called 'lightning nests'.

In 1881 my forebears unwittingly settled in a lightning nest when they chose the fertile Callide Valley in central Queensland as a site for a homestead and cattle-grazing enterprise. After a series of violent storms deluged their first camp they christened the valley the 'Dale of Thor', after the thunder god of their Norwegian homeland. Eventually, the name was abbreviated for convenience to Torsdale.

As a small child in the time before television I spent several happy years in the Dale of Thor. Early one hot summer evening, while flashes of lightning illuminated the darkness beyond the verandah and thunder rumbled in the distance, my grandfather John sat me on the arm of his squatter's chair and told me about

Thor, his magic hammer Mjillnir and the two giant goats who pull his flaming chariot through the sky. Thor's life seems to have been an endless battle with the giants of ice and frost who were always at war with the gods in Asgard.

My favourite tale was the story of the evil frost giant Thrym who stole and buried Thor's hammer, offering to return it only in exchange for the love goddess Freya. A deputation of gods arrives at Freya's palace hoping to persuade her to give herself to Thrym. It is a forlorn hope. Freya, a warrior who led the army of the Valkyrs onto the battlefield, flew into such a rage that her necklace burst. She reminded them that she was already happily married, and even if she wasn't there was no way she was going to crawl between icy sheets with some ugly frost giant.

It took the gods a while to come up with plan B.

Plan B was for Thor to get dressed up in Freya's clothes, and a thick wedding veil, and present himself as the bride-to-be. Loki, the trickster Fire God offered to be his handmaiden. By the time the cross-dressed pair arrive at Thrym's, the party's in full swing and the mead is flowing freely. 'Freya' impresses the giants by drinking three barrels in quick succession then some-what unsteadily making her way to the banquet table, where she eats an entire ox, several huge salmon, and most of the cakes and sweets on offer.

Thrym watches, speechless with astonishment until Loki tells him that the girl's so filled with desire and anticipation that she hasn't been able to eat for a week. This makes Thrym very excited indeed, but when he walks over to embrace his intended, he's disturbed by the fiery red glow of her eyes underneath her veil. 'Burning with passion for you,' Loki whispers into the giant's cold ear.

The moment of truth comes when the drunken Thrym brings in Mjillnir with much ceremony and lays it tenderly in 'Freya's' lap. The *Saga* describes the final outcome:

> 'Bear in the hammer to plight the maid; upon
> her lap the bruiser lay,
> and firmly plight our hands and fay.'
> The Thunderer's soul smiled
> in his breast; when the hammer hard on his
> lap was placed, Thrym
> first, the King of the Thursi, he slew, then
> slaughtered all the giant crew.

Sanskrit scriptures tell how the thunderbolt thrown by Lord Indra struck down the dragon Vrtra who held the waters of the world imprisoned. The thunderbolt is the sceptre, the insignia and the reality of power. According to the *Rig Veda*, the divine artisan Tvastr used his magic lathe to turn 'the well-made golden thunderbolt with its thousand spikes' with which Indra performed his heroic deeds.

Less elaborate examples of this metal object remain part of Buddhist and Tantric ritual. They're known as Vajras or diamond sceptres. The diamond sceptre is the symbol of the thunder of Buddha's doctrine which shatters false belief and mundane wickedness. The lightning that accompanies it is the illumination of *Satori*, the quicksilver flash of enlightenment which for a brief second offers a glimpse of the reality that lies hidden behind the veil of Illusion. And then it's gone. Hence the haiku 'Satori' by the Zen poet, Kakei.

> I bowed before the Buddha, now obscure,
> Now bright with lightning on the stormy
> moor.

There are several other famous thunderbolt implements and power objects. In his *Aeneid,* Virgil describes how the Cyclopes forged an iron thunderbolt for Zeus. 'Three rays of twisted hail they added to it, three of watery cloud, three of ruddy flame and the winged southern wind.' The Cyclopes were, according to Greek mythology, three of the first beings in the universe. Their names were Arges, 'Dazzling light'; Brontes, 'Thunder'; and Steropes, 'Lightning'. These were the gifts they presented to Zeus to thank him for freeing them from the Titan's underworld prison. Writes Hesiod in his *Theogeny*: 'And they remembered to be grateful to him for his kindness, and gave him thunder and the glowing thunderbolt and lightning: for before that, huge Earth had hidden these. In them (Zeus) trusts and rules over mortals and immortals.'

Zeus' consort Hera was the first lady of the universe. But Zeus was often away consorting with nymphs and the occasional mortal. When he took a fancy to the Greek princess Semele, he promised to grant her any wish if she would sleep with him. Hera got wind of this and insinuated herself into the body of Beroe, Semele's servant and confidante. She had a great idea for a wish, she told Semele: 'Tell Zeus that you want him to take you exactly as he takes Hera'. Unable to break his promise Zeus appeared in Semele's boudoir in a flaming chariot with his hands full of thunder and lightning. And not just his hands. When he entered her in the form of a lightning bolt she burst into flames and was burnt to ashes. Watching from the cover of a cloud, Hera smiled.

Thunderstorms are frequent in the mountains of Japan.

The Japanese thunder god Raiden (*Rai*, thunder and *den*, lightning), a red-skinned demon with long claws, saved Japan from a Mongol invasion in 1274. Sitting in a cloud he rained down a shower of lightning bolts that demolished the Mongol fleet, leaving only three survivors. His offsider Raiju, the 'Thunder

Animal', is a four-legged weasel-like creature that gets excited by storms, jumping from tree to tree. Trees damaged by lightning are said to have been scratched by Raiju's claws. Raiju is fond of sleeping in human navels, so many Japanese sleep on their stomach during storms just to be on the safe side.

Thunder and lightning were not always malevolent. Carved greenstone figures of Tlaloc, the Aztec rain god, show him holding a lightning symbol in the form of a golden serpent. In common with the Mayan Deity Hurakan and the Greek Zeus, Tlaloc manifested himself in three forms: as the lightning flash, the thunderbolt or thunderstone, and the sound of thunder. It was with a lightning bolt that Tlaloc split open the rock that held the first grain of maize imprisoned within it. Each lightning flash that illuminated the Aztec cornfields was seen by farmers as a blessing, a reminder of the original act of creation.

Chinese Taoists associate lightning with fertility and procreation. An ancient prayer invokes the image: 'As the powerful and resistless thunderbolt cleaves the cloud to turn it into rain, so open this woman's womb so that she may soon give birth.'

In central Australia, thunder is the voice of Baiame, the Father-of-All, who created a special instrument so that his voice could be heard at rituals and men's initiation ceremonies. It's called a bullroarer and if you've ever heard a bull bellowing in rage and frustration, then it's easy to understand why.

The bullroarer is a small flat blade of wood or bone carved into an elongated pointed oval shape with a long piece of string threaded through a hole at one end. Holding the free end of the string, the player whirls the blade in fast rhythmic swings. The spinning blade also rotates on its axis creating a deep eerie hum whose volume and pitch increase in intensity in proportion to the speed at which it is whirled. When several are used at once, the resulting sound compels attention and awe.

Baiame's first prototype was not a success because it was made of stone and was too heavy for men to lift. Inspiration came when Baiame was chopping firewood energetically in the forests of Sky-land. Chips flew in all directions. Now and then one would spin through the air vibrating with a humming sound that varied with the speed and size of the splinter.

After a few experiments and modifications, Baiame was satisfied. He called the instrument *Gayandi* and brought it down to Earth to give to men. He showed them how to make the first 'Bora' ring, the sacred circle on the ground that recreates the circular path of the bullroarer through the air. He told the elders to treat his inventions with great reverence, to hide them when not in use, and showed the old men how to whirl them when they wanted to hear him speak.

The ritual use of the bullroarer to mimic the voice of thunder is part of the practice of 'imitative' magic based on the principle that like attracts like. Its prehistoric roots identify it as one of the oldest musical instruments to remain in use in its original form. One carved from reindeer horn was discovered in a cave in the Dordogne district in France, while Paleolithic rock paintings in several parts of Africa depict men whirling bullroarers at ceremonies connected with rain-making. In ancient Greece, the sound of the bullroarer accompanied the revelation of the Dionysian mysteries. Its Greek name, *Rombos*, survives in the French term for the instrument. In other parts of Europe it's known as the 'thunderspell' or 'thunderbolt'.

The question arises—how did the bullroarer come to all of these various cultures? Or did each develop the concept separately and in isolation? Indigenous Australians, for instance, have been separated from the rest of the world for 100,000 years. Did their holy men tap into the memory bank of The Akasha where the knowledge of the Universe lies concealed from all but initiates?

Doug Boyd was commissioned by the American-based Menninger Foundation in 1972 to report on the extraordinary powers displayed by a native

American leader and medicine man named, appropriately, Rolling Thunder. Boyd's book of the same name has already achieved the status of a classic in its field.

One passage describes how Rolling Thunder brings down a lightning strike while Boyd kneels, watching closely.

> Rolling Thunder was holding a tiny stick and he was poking at an ordinary stink bug. He looked at me and his face loosened for a moment.
>
> 'This will bring the rain.'
>
> He herded the big black bug about, tapping on its back to make it run and on its head to make it turn.
>
> 'Now watch!'
>
> He quickly flipped the stick. The bug landed on its back, righted itself and nearly stood on its head with its back end in the air. There was a loud, sharp crack: a bolt of lightning, a bright, clearly defined zigzag line.
>
> 'You see? This brings the lightning!'
>
> Again and again the act was repeated and again and again the lightning came. It was unbelievable. I had never seen such lightning.

Loud and clear, right overhead, always in the same place, the bolts came in rapid succession. It seemed to be synchronized precisely with the agitations of the bug. I might have been watching someone scratching a screwdriver on a battery pole or touching two live wires together. It became apparent as it continued that this was an uncommon but natural phenomenon produced by a real cause-and-effect relationship.

'This brings the lightning. You tease him and it brings the lightning. His irritation stimulates the lightning and that's what brings the rain.'

The lightning bolts continued to come one after the other. Rising up on his haunches, Rolling Thunder jumped in a low, crouching stoop, his arm extended to reach the bug with the stick. He continued the pushing and flipping, accompanied now by a throaty cry: 'Heagh, heaghhh . . .'

Rolling Thunder says that he aligns himself with the Great Spirit who is the source of all energy. Taoist and Tibetan shamans say the same thing. About such phenomena, the yoga master Swami Rama once observed, 'every man can have his own hypothesis but he still has to account for the facts'.

Thunderstones are ritual objects used by rain-makers and priests since prehistoric times. The Incas believed that the Sky God Ataguju made thunder and lightning by hurling stones from his sling. These small stones were revered as charms that made fields fertile and protected their owners from lightning. The amulets were also 'capable of kindling the dangerous flames of desire in the most frigid bosoms'.

French farmers carry thunderstones in their pockets to ward off lightning. They call them 'Pierre de tonnerre' (which translates as 'thunder rock'). Siberian Yakut peoples call thunderstones *Ätin Sugätä*. Not only are they protective talismans, powder from these stones is used in traditional medicines.

Anthropologists and cultural historians thought that thunderstones were either pieces of meteorite or objects of 'primitive superstition'. The naturalist Tallius, writing in 1649, attempted the first 'scientific' explanation. Thunderstones, he said, 'are generated in the sky by fularous exhalation conglobed in a cloud by the circumfused humour'. It was not very helpful.

Thunderstones, thunderbolts, sky axes, lightning arrowheads and other such talismans are neither stones nor meteorites. And they do not fall from the sky. They are composed of a substance called 'fulgurite', derived from the Latin 'fulgur' meaning 'lightning.' Fulgurites are formed when lightning strikes a desert, beach or sandy soil, where the sand contains a high proportion of quartz. The extreme heat of the lightning blast (86,000°F or 30,000°C) fuses the sand into long glass-like tubes moulded round the form of the lightning. Each fulgurite is a cast of a lightning flash. The longest recorded measures 4.6 metres (15 feet).

These power objects can be found in shops that sell crystals and rock specimens. At the time of writing, there was a 53 centimetre-long (21 inches) fulgurite from Indiana for sale on eBay for US$261.87. If it can kindle the flame of desire in even the most frigid bosom as well as protecting your home from lightning, it might just be worth it.

# The Path of the Rainbow

They climbed out of the earth; and still climbing,
rose above it. They were in the rainbow. Far abroad,
over ocean and land, they could see through its
transparent walls the earth beneath their feet. Stairs
beside stairs wound up together, and beautiful
beings of all ages climbed along with them. They
knew they were going up to the country whence
the shadows fall.

George MacDonald
*The Golden Key*

Water paints with rich pigments. Trees and plants, flowers and fruit, animals, birds and reptiles, the sky and sea that colour our world are water's creation. Whether rainbows are water's artworks, bridges to paradise, giant serpents or the logical result of refracted light, they never lose their capacity to enchant us with their ephemeral beauty.

The eyes through which we see have lenses of water named after the rainbow sylph, Iris. Iris is the Greek handmaiden of Hera, the Queen of Heaven. Her main task is to keep the clouds filled with rain, but that's not all. She also helps mortals avoid a lingering death by flying down, severing their last tenuous ties with earthly existence, and leading them up her rainbow into paradise.

This mysterious arc of light that links earth and sky is the perennial symbol of the bridge that connects our material world to that which lies 'somewhere over the rainbow'. Across this bridge pass deities, heroes and mortals, some coming, some going. Perhaps the best known is Bifrost, a pivotal element in Scandinavian myth. A fusion of the elements, air and water, Bifrost is the magic path that connects Asgard, the home of the gods, with Midgard, the world of men.

Asgard is vulnerable to attack from aggressive frost giants, so a divine sentinel named Heimdall guards the end of the rainbow against unwanted visitors. It's a demanding job, but Heimdall has extraordinary gifts. He can see what's happening for a hundred miles around and his hearing is so acute that he can hear new grass shoots pushing up through the soil and wool growing on the backs of sheep.

Heimdall has a powerful alarm in the form of Gjallar, a magic horn so loud it can be heard throughout the universe. Thus protected Bifrost will remain secure until the time of Ragnorok, the Norse apocalypse. Then, according to the Eddic prophecy, Heimdall will blow Gjallar one last time to summon all the gods to do battle with the fire giant Surt and his evil host who surge across Bifrost. Under their combined weight the rainbow bridge will finally collapse.

The Japanese rainbow is another Heavenly Floating Bridge. Its custodian is Izume, the dancing goddess of happiness in the Japanese Dreamtime, who saved the world from eternal darkness by performing a spectacular celestial striptease.

Once there was a terrible row between the bad tempered storm deity Susano and the gentle sun goddess, Amatersu. At the end of her emotional tether, Amatersu retreated into a deep cave, barricading the entrance with great boulders and leaving the world in darkness.

This was a serious matter. Eight hundred gods met on the banks of the Heaven River to work out how to coax Amatersu out of hiding. Finally it was Omoigame, 'He of Great Wisdom', who came up with the most original plan. He instructed the Heavenly Jeweller to fabricate an exquisite necklace of stars, while the Divine Coppersmith was set to work making a great polished mirror. The necklace and mirror were hung, along with brightly coloured ribbons, precious stones and prayer scrolls on the shrubs and trees surrounding the mouth of the cave. It was an impressive tribute and the gods gathered round to admire it.

Then Omoigane asked Uzume to dance for the assembled gathering, commanding them to applaud loudly and enthusiastically. Uzume began with an undulating motion that increased in tempo as the gods clapped and cheered. She whirled faster and faster until, one by one, her clothes fell away. Nude, she performed an original and lascivious dance that brought the house down.

Inside the cave Amatersu wondered what on earth could be happening out there. How could everyone have such fun when the world was in darkness? In the end, curiosity got the better of her. Rolling aside one of the boulders, she emerged from the cave in a sunburst of radiant light and was momentarily taken aback by her image reflected in the great burnished copper mirror. At once, the Strong God seized her, while others strung a rope across the entrance to the cave to prevent her going back. Then the multitude pleaded with her never to leave them again. Slowly Amatersu let herself be persuaded to stay, and the sun shone once more.

The Court of Heaven punished the storm god by fining him a hefty sum, cutting off his beard, toenails and fingernails and banishing him from Heaven to live forever on earth. As a reward for her command performance, Izume was made guardian of the Heavenly Bridge. At her feet flows the Spring of Immortality whose waters she dispenses to all who pass on their way to the Other World. Because her mortal priests use imitations of this water to brew herbal medicines, the shrines of Izume are hallowed places of healing and comfort for those in sickness and distress.

Polynesian people tell how Ina of the Moon took a handsome mortal lover up to her celestial home. After many happy years together, Ina said to him, 'You are bending with age and infirmity; soon death must claim you for you are a native of earth. But this home of mine must never know the defilement of death; we must embrace and part. Return to earth and there end your days.' Then Ina caused a rainbow to span the heavens, and down it her aged and disconsolate lover reluctantly made his way back to the mortal world.

In the myths of Paleolithic and Neolithic peoples and present-day religions in Africa, Oceania and the Americas, the rainbow is equated with the celestial serpent, the Great Father of All Things. In the myths of indigenous Java, the rainbow is a two-headed snake— one head drinks in the water of the northern ocean while the other vomits it back into the Southern Sea.

The Rainbow Snake who creates the world and brings rain is the common totemic ancestor of many of the world's indigenous peoples. The Egyptians worshipped him in the form of Atum, the serpent who emerges from the primeval waters to spit the whole of creation into being. At the end of time Atum will revert to his divine incarnation. When nothing is left, he tells Osiris in *The Book of the Dead*, 'I am he who remains . . . the earth shall return to formless chaos, and then I shall transform myself into a serpent which no man knows and no god sees'.

African peoples envisage the rainbow as a great python. Semang Negritos tell their children that from time to time he slithers into the sky to take a bath. The water on his scales gleams brightly. 'When he tips his bathwater out,' they say, 'it falls to earth as sun-rain, a water most perilous to humans.'

The South African journal of Bishop Callaway contains the story of Utshintsha, a Zulu Christian and his encounter with the much feared rainbow.

Utshintsha had been working in his garden during a shower of rain. When it cleared, he said: 'There descended into the river a rainbow. I ran away when I saw the rainbow moving towards me, dazzling my eyes with a red colour . . . Men say "the rainbow is a disease. If it rests on a man something will happen to him". After the rainbow drove me from the garden, my body became as it is now, affected with swellings.' The bishop noted that his patient had 'a scaly eruption over his whole body'.

Further north, the Ewe people see in the rainbow the reflected image of the great snake Anyiewo seeking water in the clouds. He lives in a giant termite mound. If he falls on any person he devours them, so anthills and rainbows are both treated with dread.

The Incas dared not look at rainbows; they covered their mouths with their hands in respect, for this was the feathered crown of Illapa who brought rain and thunder. The *Books of the Inca* explain how the feathers of Illapa's crown came to be coloured by the blood of the Rainbow Serpent: 'When it was no more than a little worm it was nourished by mortals but it ate so greedily that it grew to an enormous size. Then the mortals were forced to kill it because it demanded human hearts for food. Birds dipped their feathers in its blood and their plumage was dyed with the bright colours of the rainbow.'

The rainbows that arch across the skies of West Africa are the work of an extraordinary deity, one who can change colour at will. It all began with a competition between two creatures who acted as intermediaries and messengers for the Great Sky Father, bringing his wisdom and knowledge down to earth.

One was the Spider God, Anansi.

After spinning the entire world into being at Sky Father's request Anansi endowed humans with many gifts. He showed people how to pound corn in a mortar to make flour, how to use fire for cooking; he taught, too, the art of telling sacred stories that could touch the heart.

Anansi's rival was Chameleon, the master of lightning and storm. Chameleon's power was recognised even in Europe. A magic recipe from a Grimoire, or book of spells, from the Middle Ages tells how 'the head and gullet of a chameleon burned with oak give command of thunder and rain'.

One day as Chameleon was walking past a great tree, he heard rustling muttering sounds coming from inside the trunk. Splitting it open with a bolt of lightning, Chameleon released the first water which divided and spread in rivers and oceans across the earth. Out of this water came the first beings, the ancestors of humans.

Tired of competing with one another, Anansi and Chameleon, both masters of shape shifting, agreed that whoever could manifest the most magnificent form would be the victor.

Anansi began by becoming the yellow of a tiger's eye; his adversary copied him exactly. So Anansi transformed himself into the blue sky reflected in a clear pool of water, then into the grey membrane of a lizard's eye, then the pink blood vessel in an antelope's ear. But each time Chameleon matched his skill. When Anansi displayed the shimmering iridescence of a drop of dew suspended in a spider's web, Chameleon responded by combining all of the previous colours into a giant rainbow and painting it triumphantly across the sky. Defeated, Anansi quietly wove a silken cord and descended to earth, leaving Chameleon as Sky Father's only go-between, the Rainbow Messenger.

The Bakongo of Zaire address the rainbow as Lubangala, the Protector who shields the clan from the thunderstorms that blow in from the Atlantic. They see a coloured giant arching his body over their village to protect it as a mother guards her child from hyenas.

In central Australia the rainbow is the dutiful son of the rain, anxious to prevent his father from falling down. If a rainbow appears in the sky before enough rain has fallen then it must be driven away by the performance of an elaborate ritual. The rainmaker paints his quartz rain stones with red ochre and throws water over them and himself. Then he paints three small rainbows: one on the ground, one on his body and one on a shield marked with jagged white lines representing lightning. The shield is hidden in a secure place, imprisoning the spirit of the rainbow and keeping it out of the sky until the rain has fallen.

The rainbow is both a symbol of transfiguration and an affirmation of divinity.

After the Great Flood had abated, Yahweh promised Noah that he wouldn't do it again. The rainbow is a visible sign of that promise. 'I set my bow in the cloud,' said Yahweh, 'and it shall be a sign of the covenant between me and the earth. When I bring clouds over the earth and the bow is seen in the clouds, I will remember my covenant which is between me and you and every living creature.' Western religious artists often portray Christ seated on a throne in the midst of a rainbow. In John's *Revelation*, when the doors of heaven opened 'there was a rainbow round the throne'.

Tibetan Buddhism teaches that the 'rainbow body' is the highest state attainable in the realm of *Samsāra* before one is infused with the clear light of *Nirvāna*. Rainbows appear when an enlightened being dies or is cremated. On the day that Tsondr Rinpoche left this world at Dolanji in Tibet in 1985, the district was suffused with rainbows. According to an eyewitness, some were straight as well as round, some white and others five-coloured. 'They appeared out of a clear sky as he died. Even when it was nearly dark there were white rainbows glowing in the sky.' After the death of such a man, it is said that the four elements that make up his body dissolve symbolically into rainbow light demonstrating the insubstantial nature of material existence.

The Iroquois, who roamed the plains that now form New York City, tell the following story of the rainbow and how it came to be.

When the earth was brought into being, Sky Woman gave birth to twins, one good and one evil. The good twin created wide rivers and high hills to guard the water's path through the valleys below. Jealous, the bad twin brought forth Sais-Tah-Go-Wa, a great serpent-like sea monster and directed it to enter the rivers and destroy them. Accustomed to the freedom of the great ocean, Sais-Tah-Go-Wa felt confined by the banks of the streams and tried to tear them further apart by writhing furiously through the water and hurling great rocks down on them as they fled towards the sea. When the good twin rushed to defend his creations from destruction, the monster tried to escape but was unable to return to the sea through the rivers he had destroyed. Afraid, he fled up into the sky.

Sun was peacefully making his way across the heavens when Sais-Tah-Go-Wa suddenly appeared in the firmament. When he learned what damage the monster had done, Sun decided that it must never be allowed to return to earth; throwing the huge snake-like being across the sky, Sun clasped him down firmly from east to west.

Quite by chance, He-no the Thunderer was passing by, riding a black storm cloud. Admiring the strength of Sais-Tah-Go-Wa and his shining scales, He-no picked him up saying, 'This will make a perfect bow for my lightning hunter', and he took the monster back to his lodge.

Sais-Tah-Go-Wa is restless in captivity and tries to escape when He-no is away directing storms; but the ever-watchful Sun who sees all catches him each time and, bending him across the sky, paints him with the brightest colours so that He-no can easily find him. When the Iroquois see the resplendent hues of the rainbow after summer showers they know that Sais-Tah-Go-Wa has escaped again. As the colours fade and the Sun shines, they say that He-no has taken him back and locked him in his lodge once more.

Irish folktales paint the rainbow as a magic portal, a bridge between the natural and the supernatural, which no human can cross except in his imagination. When gods ascend this fragile arch they must leave behind their heavy golden armour in a pile at the rainbow's end for any mortal lucky enough to find it.

Unfortunately, we can never recover the treasure because, scientists tell us, the end of the rainbow is impossible to find. The vision of the rainbow is determined by the position of the observer, which means that each of us sees our own unique personal perspective. As we move, so does the bow, and the pot of gold remains forever beyond our reach.

The first person to intuit this was Theodoric, a Dominican monk who, in 1304, used a large glass globe filled with water to simulate a giant raindrop. Exposing it to sunlight, Theodoric was able to demonstrate how, when the sun's rays illuminate the drop, most pass straight through but the light at the outer edges is refracted (or bent) by the convex surface into the colours of the spectrum. These are then reflected by the inner concave surface back through the outer surface, where the rays are bent once more as they exit. Each raindrop, therefore, contains the potentiality of the entire rainbow. Theodoric's next observation was just as remarkable. He noticed that from any one viewpoint only one colour was visible. When he moved, even slightly, other colours appeared. From this Theodoric deduced that each rainbow colour comes from a different set of drops and this being so, the rainbow was the consequence of millions of raindrops, each reflecting a particular colour to the observer.

When colours of different wavelengths are refracted at differing angles, the separation of the spectrum occurs. This combination of the same colours emerging at slightly differing angles from every one of a million raindrops gives us the vision of several distinct bands of colour. If that's not worthy of reverence and awe I don't know what is.

In the 1600s, Rene Descartes determined mathematically that when two refractions and one reflection are involved, a rainbow is only visible at an angle of 42 degrees from the path of the sun's rays. Isaac Newton, experimenting with glass prisms in 1666, showed that each colour of the spectrum has its own optimal angle of refraction. Using a second prism to recapture the colours divided by the first, Newton was able to merge them back together into white light, thus demonstrating for the first time that white light is a composite of all the other colours.

Every rainbow is a segment of an imaginary circle whose centre is the shadow of the observer's head. For this reason we seldom get to see the complete circle except from the top of a high mountain or by looking down from an aircraft window. Circular rainbows often appear above the vortex of great waterfalls.

Sometimes, if you're lucky, you'll even see circular spectra in the spray of a garden hose.

In his treatise on *Problems in the Field of Optics and the Rainbow* (1567), Francesco Maurolico asks: 'What, then, in optics is most difficult of demonstration? Is it not, perhaps, the explanation of the form, size, and colour of the rainbow, seeing that there enters into its production a consideration of the entire field of optics, namely vision, light, reflection and transparent bodies concerning which many have written; but no one has as yet given a satisfactory explanation?'.

Scientific explanations relate to the mechanism by which a rainbow becomes visible. They do not account for its creation. It's like trying to describe the subject of a photograph, a landscape for instance, by studying the mechanism of the camera. They are two different things. One does not explain the other. Nevertheless, meteorologists insist that rainbows are just the result of sunlight falling on a veil of raindrops, or more specifically, the light of the sun (or moon) 'dispersed into the spectral colours by refractions and reflections inside the transparent raindrops'.

That doesn't account for the childlike sense of joy and wonder we feel when we look up and marvel at the rainbow's beauty and symmetry. Something else is happening besides 'reflections and refractions', something that inspires profound thought, and its most creative expression, poetry.

After dinner on the evening of Friday 26 March 1802, William Wordsworth retired to his study leaving his family sitting talking round the fire. Suddenly, inspiration seized him and he began to write:

> My heart leaps up when I behold
>> A rainbow in the sky:
> So was it when my life began;
> So is it now I am a man;
> So be it when I shall grow old
>> Or let me die.

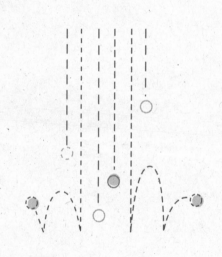

# Hail—The Wrath of the Gods

I wield the flail of the lashing hail
And whiten the green plants under
And then again I dissolve it in rain
And laugh as I pass in thunder.

Percy Bysshe Shelley
*The Cloud*

Who is this deity who wields the flail? Is it a God or a demon? Is hail divine vengeance, or is it the consequence of particular atmospheric conditions? Can hail be called, controlled, diverted or dissolved and, if so, how and by whom?

These were hotly debated questions in times past. Answers varied from culture to culture but all unanimously agreed that, whether it was created by the action of God, nature, or humans with special powers, hail was definitely a curse.

The God of the Old Testament used hail as a weapon. Time after time he asserts his ownership and control of hail. In Job, for instance, the Lord talks about 'the storehouses of the hail which I reserve for times of trouble, for days of war and battle'. Sometimes hail was used to punish doubters and unbelievers as in Haggai: 'I struck all the work of your hands with blight, mildew and hail, yet you did not turn to me'; and 'hail will sweep away your refuge' (Isaiah). When the Amorite armies fled from Joshua 'the Lord hurled large hailstones down on them from the sky, and more died from the hailstones than were killed by the swords of the Israelites'.

In the Book of Revelation, Christ's vision as revealed by John, hail is the final punishment, the seventh bowl of the Wrath of God, poured out on the sinners of Babylon: 'huge hailstones of a hundred pounds each fell upon men. And they cursed God on account of the plague because the plague was so terrible'. The most compelling demonstration of biblical hail-making was performed by Moses to persuade Pharaoh to release the Israelites from bondage. Moses warns Pharaoh, but he doesn't respond.

'Stretch out your hand towards the sky,' whispers the Lord to Moses, 'so that hail will fall all over Egypt.' Moses does as he is told and 'thunder and hail and lightning flashed down to the ground . . . It was the worst storm in all the land of Egypt . . . hail struck everything in the fields—both men and animals; it beat down everything growing in the fields and stripped every tree . . .' When the pharaoh concedes defeat, Moses spreads out his arms towards the sky and the thunder and hail cease. It was certainly a very impressive demonstration. Did it really happen? Was the Lord responsible or was Moses, as some would have it, a great shaman who could utter the 'words of power' that compelled the heavens, and the waters to do his bidding?

The belief that the weather in general, and hail in particular, could be controlled by magic spells, rituals and incantations has been with us from antiquity. The first-century Roman poet Lucan describes how the witches of Thessaly called down thunder and lightning and then, with spells, dispersed them. The Teutonic legal code, the *Lex Visigothorum* (700 AD) provides severe penalties for those who use spells and incantations to bring down hailstorms on fields and vineyards. In 1326, a French friar was put on trial at Avenon for 'having provoked thunder, lightning, tempests and hailstorms'.

The Tantric science of *Mantras*, or Words of Power, based on the Law of Vibration articulated in the Mantrayãna discipline of yoga, teaches that there is associated with every creature, each object and element of nature, a particular level of vibration. When formulated as a *Mantra* and spoken by a perfected practitioner, these sound vibrations are capable of disintegrating the object or element. In the case of lesser deities, such as hail gods, they can impel and command obedience.

One tale in the annals of Tibetan tantra is that of Milarepa, the Enlightened One, whose biography, *The Jesun Kahbum*, is one of the sacred books of the East. Milarepa starts out as a practitioner of black magic then, overcome by remorse, he converts to Buddhism and becomes a realised Master. The turning point in his life is the creation of a massive hailstorm. Briefly, his story begins when, disinherited by his sly uncle and aunt, the young Milarepa promises his widowed mother that he will study the art of sorcery in order to punish the greedy relatives and their family.

Milarepa is guided to a tantric master who teaches

him the art of launching hail storms and guiding them with the tips of his fingers. Milarepa waits until the barley crop of his uncle is about to be harvested. He erects his apparatus and chants the requisite charm on a hill overlooking the fertile valley, but nothing happens. 'I struck the Earth with my folded robe and wept bitterly,' he says. Then huge black clouds gather in the sky and when they coalesce, 'there burst from it a violent hailstorm which destroyed every single ear of grain in the fields. Three falls of hail followed in succession and cut deep gorges in the hillsides. The country folk thus deprived of their harvest, set up one great wail of distress and grief.' Overcome, Milarepa repents and converts to Buddhism.

Hail was, and is, a serious threat to peasant agriculture. It can destroy the food supply for an entire community in a matter of minutes. It is easy to understand why people would want to stop hail if they could, or look for someone to blame if they couldn't.

While the control of hail may have once been the province of the Lord, by the Middle Ages it had mysteriously become the plaything of the Devil—or at least so said the Dominican Inquisitors when they declared war on witchcraft in the fifteenth century. The doctors of the Inquisition relied for their information on certain reference texts that dealt with the finer points of witchcraft and its detection.

Chapter 34 of *The Book of All Forbidden Arts, Unbelief and Sorcery* (1455) begins with the warning: 'To make hail and sudden shower is one of these (black) arts for he that will meddle therewith must not only give himself to the devil, but deny God, holy baptism and all Christian grace'.

There are interviews with imprisoned 'witches' who will not (or cannot) reveal to the author, a Doctor Hartleib, the actual process by which hail is made. He offers to spare the life of one if only she will tell him her secret, but to no avail.

Another tool of the Inquisition was 'The Witches Hammer,' the *Malleus Malifecarum* (1486). It offers more detail on 'how witches raise and stir up hail-storms and tempests and cause lightning to blast both men and beasts'. One of the guilty 'hail-raisers' documented in the *Malleus* is Agnes who, after torture, reveals details of her eighteen-year relationship with a friendly demon. One day around noon the demon comes to Agnes' house and asks her to bring a jug of water out to the plain nearby. There Agnes meets the devil himself waiting patiently under a tree. She is instructed to dig a hole in the ground and pour the water into it. Then she stirs the water with her finger 'in the name of the devil and all the other demons'. The water disappears and the devil rises up to produce a hailstorm that devastates the fields of Agnes' angry neighbours who subsequently denounce her.

Two hundred years later, the *Compendium Malifi-carum*, an ecclesiastical text of 1626, still insists that hail is made by witches: 'According to their confessions, they beat water with a wand, and then they threw into the air or into the water a certain powder which Satan had given them. By this means, a cloud was raised which afterward turned to hailstones and fell wherever the witches wished.'

In an apparent contradiction, selected members of the clergy were believed to have the power to influence the weather. Saint Francis told one congregation that the heavy hailstorms that devastated their fields were God's punishment for their sins and if they didn't repent, he warned, the wrath of God would be redoubled against them. The saint's biblical reference for his sermon was, of course, the magic of Moses.

There were almost as many ways to combat hail as there were to make it. In ancient Rome, hail-guards appointed by the Senate alerted the public when the first green-tinted hail clouds appeared on the horizon. When the alarm sounded, people offered sacrifices of chickens and lambs to propitiate the storm spirits. Those too poor to own lambs and chickens pricked their index fingers and offered up their blood by way of atonement for any offence they may have given.

In sixteenth-century Spain rural folk hired 'cloud-chasers' to conjure away hail-bearing clouds. This service in South African Zulu communities is performed by the Shepherds of Heaven, the Heaven-herds. Heaven-herds are not rainmakers. They intercede with the Lord-of-the-Sky to drive away lightning, hail and violent thunderstorms.

One has to be called by the Sky to become a Heaven-herd; being struck by lightning and surviving is regarded as a powerful indicator of divine approval; having one's house struck but not damaged is another. Heaven-herds are initiated into their art in the period between the first new moon and the full moon. The final test is a practical demonstration. When a violent storm appears, the novice must perform his rituals. If he succeeds in diverting the thunder and hail, then he is accepted into the guild of Heaven-herds.

In *The Golden Yoke, The Legal Cosmology of Buddhist Tibet*, Rebecca Redwood French devotes a chapter to The Hail Protector of the Crystal Fortress. The Crystal Fort is a castle in the remote district of Shelkar; the head lama of the nearby monastery is the hereditary hail protector of the area which is prone to severe storms. Entering the monastery at the age of eight, the child was taught how to perform the annual cycle of rituals necessary to keep hail at bay. At 22, he began his official duties, funded by an annual hail protection tax paid by the local people.

At the beginning of the growing season the lama begins to recite age-old mystical prayers and chants in a small hut in the midst of the barley fields. His devotions are directed to Mahakala, the Great Black One, the master of hail in the Tibetan Buddhist hierarchy of protective deities. He wears a tiger-skin loincloth on his black body, has a round face with three eyes, a snarling mouth, and snakes in his hair. Surrounded by an aura of brilliant yellow flames, Mahakala wears garlands of freshly severed heads around his neck and waist; his six hands carry thunderbolts and choppers. Tibet has many hail-protectors who've been propitiating Mahakala for hundreds, even thousands, of years. Their reputation depends on their ability and effectiveness. It's not a job that allows for frequent failure, so the continuing presence of such people into the modern era seems to indicate a high success rate.

European clergy were not so fortunate. The ritual exorcism of hail included prayers that implored God and his angels to overcome the infernal powers of darkness. The consecrated host was taken to the church door, where the priest made the sign of the cross with it in the direction of the storm. If this was not effective, the priest was blamed. Some were even stoned by angry farmers. During a modern procession to banish a hailstorm at Mont-Saxonnex in the

French Alps, someone called out to the person carrying the crucifix, 'Hold Him up high, so He can see all the damage he is doing'.

Noise is another deterrent. The clashing of metal pots and pans, fireworks, shouting, the beating of drums and gongs or the tolling of bells, all have been used to scare away hail demons. Even now some parishes employ teams of bellringers during the hail season in the grape growing districts of France, Italy and Spain. Many old bells were engraved with appropriate inscriptions such as *'Tempestatum fugo, nubes fugo'*—I make the storm and clouds flee.

The firing of guns and cannon as a protective measure persisted into the twentieth century. British scientists advised farmers that shooting debris at the clouds with special anti-hail guns would be effective. It wasn't. Instead, people were injured by falling pellets. In 1902, 11 people were killed by hail-guns in Austria alone. Nevertheless, as late as 1965, the journal *Weather* reported that anti-hail rockets were still being used in northern Italy, Austria and Kenya.

What is this substance that threatens humans, animals and crops alike, and how is it formed? In his *Natural History* (77 AD) Pliny asserts that hail is rain frozen by the action of winds, while the *Meteorologica* of Aristotle (384–322 BC) devotes two chapters to speculations about the nature and origin of hail.

Aristotle concludes that snow and hail are similar, differing only in size and shape.

Scientifically speaking both men were correct.

Hail starts to form when strong vertical air currents move rapidly upward in warm weather. The overheated air lifts large raindrops into the cooler atmosphere where they are frozen into ice crystals. As these become heavier they drop, only to be lifted once more by high-speed updrafts, before they drop again. This process is repeated many times, building up concentric layers of ice similar in cross-section to the rings of an onion. Eventually the 'stones' become so heavy that they fall to earth. Hail can vary in size from tiny balls to large ice cannonballs.

The mechanics of hailstone creation were observed at close quarters by Lieutenant-Colonel William Rankin, a jet pilot in the United States Air Force in 1959 who was forced to bale out when his engine failed while trying to fly above a large thunderstorm. The outside temperature was −50°C and Rankin was wearing only a lightweight summer flying suit when he ejected and drifted down into the storm below.

'A massive blast of air jarred me from head to toe,' he recalled. 'I went soaring up and up and up. I saw that I was in an angry ocean of boiling clouds—blacks and greys and whites, spilling over one another, into one another, digesting one another!' Rankin felt himself blown in many directions—'up, down, sideways, clockwise, counter-clockwise over and over again'—accompanied by hailstones undergoing a similar ordeal. Bruised and battered by the hail and the erratic and forceful movement of the air currents, Rankin closed his eyes. 'This was nature's bedlam,' he thought, 'a black cageful of screaming lunatics, beating me with big flat sticks, roaring at me, trying to crush me.'

Rankin survived. When he finally reached the ground he looked at his watch. It was 6.40 pm and he had ejected at 6.05 pm. He had been in the storm for 35 minutes. Rankin recovered and returned to flying, but other aviators have not been so lucky. In 1930, the bodies of five men encased in layers of ice fell out of a hail cloud on the Rhone Mountains in Germany. Human hailstones if you like. They were five amateur glider pilots who, sucked into the cloud by strong air currents, had bailed out and suffered the conse-quences. Other strange hailstones have been recorded. One contained a large gopher turtle which had no business up there at 50,000 feet.

The more severe the storm the bigger the hail, because the high upward velocity of the winds holds hailstones aloft longer in the hail-growing region of the storm. St John's 45 kilogram (100 pound) hail-stones in *The Book of Revelations* have some modern equivalents. *Scientific American* magazine tells of a single massive hailstone weighing around 36 kilograms (80 pounds) that fell near Santa Fe in 1882. It was preserved in sawdust and exhibited to crowds of spectators until it melted.

In 1953, 50 giant ice blocks each weighing around 75 kilograms (165 pounds) dropped out of a clear sky at Long Beach, California. Fortunately, no-one was injured. But the biggest block of ice ever to fall to earth landed in the backyard of an astonished farmer in Rosshire, Great Britain, on 13 August 1849. 'After a loud thunderclap,' reported *The Times*, 'a large and irregular-shaped mass of ice, reckoned to be nearly 20 feet in circumference and of a proportionate thickness, fell near the farmhouse.' The ice had a beautiful crystalline transparency formed by a mass of multi-faceted crystals coalesced together. Was this hailstone from outer space? Being clear and without the mass of oxygen bubbles that give common hail its white appearance, the great iceblock of 1849 defied rational explanation.

Hailstones are made up of concentric layers of ice and air bubbles that resemble the structure of an onion. At the heart of each is a crystal. The comparison between onions and hail is appropriate symbolically as well as physically. The concentric pattern is one of water's signature symbols. Drop a pebble in a pond and this is water's response—a series of vibrations, ripples that move out from the centre. This is how we depict the Earth and, beyond it, the Universe.

The onion was a sacred object because its structure epitomised this cosmic pattern. Even the word 'onion' derives from the Latin *unio* meaning unity and oneness. Because it is the only vegetable that represents the essence of things, onions were thought to have a soul. The ancient Egyptians buried onions with their pharaohs as symbols of eternal life. King Ramses IV who died in 1160 BCE was embalmed with onions in his eye sockets. Next time it hails, cut some hailstones through the centre and you'll find this onion-like pattern. If you're especially favoured, you might even find something equally miraculous.

On 26 May 1907, a severe storm swept through the Vosges area of France. Abbé Gueniot was reading quietly in his presbytery at Remirmont while hail pelted down outside. Suddenly an excited neighbour knocked on his door. 'Come, Father,' he said 'and see the miracle.' The hailstones were convex, and in the centre of each was the image of a woman in a robe turned up at the bottom like that of a priest's cope.

In his evidence to an ecclesiastical inquiry into the incident, the Abbé was precise: 'I should perhaps describe it still more exactly by saying it was like the Virgin of the Hermits. The outlines of the image were slightly hollow, as though they had been formed with a punch, but were very boldly drawn.' No human agency could have been responsible, the inquiry concluded, because of the vast quantity of image-bearing hailstones and the 107 witnesses who testified to the event, which was confined to a strip of land three-quarters of a mile wide and several miles long.

In the absence of a scientific explanation, the Abbé offered his own. The Sunday of the previous week had been the feast day of the Virgin of the Hermits but the town council had, for its own reasons, cancelled the permit for the procession which was being prepared. 'On the following Sunday at the same hour,' said the Abbé triumphantly, 'the artillery of heaven caused a vertical procession which no-one could forbid!'

To the indigenous peoples of northern Australia, hailstones are eggs laid by the Rainbow Serpent. A long time ago, the story goes, a shower of hailstones fell near a group of people camped by a river. The elders had never seen those strange white stones before. When the storm had passed, they sat and watched the stones to see what would happen. The hailstones seemed to burrow slowly into the ground and disappear. Had they melted away or dug them-selves in? The elders couldn't agree.

'They must be still there,' said one. He took a digging stick and made several holes looking for evidence. When he found worms at the bottom, he announced triumphantly, 'See, here are the children of the Rainbow Serpent, already hatched out from the white eggs that fell from the sky'.

Who could argue with that?

# Snow—Hieroglyphs from Heaven

A lacy snowflake glistens in your hand. You can't help looking at it. See how it sparkles in a wonderfully intricate pattern. Then it quivers, melts and lies dead in your hand. It is no more. The snowflake, which fluttered down from infinite space onto your hand, where it sparkled and quivered and died—that is yourself. Wherever you see life—that is yourself!

Albert Schweitzer

The Zen artists and poets of Japan believe that three things represent the epitome of cosmic bliss, three signposts on the way to heaven. These three most beautiful things are the moon, cherry blossoms and snow.

Our hearts instinctively reach out to the intense whiteness of snow and the mystery that lies therein. 'White acts upon our souls like absolute silence,' wrote the artist Vassily Kandinsky. 'This silence is not something lifeless but replete with life potential . . . It is a nothingness filled with childish happiness . . . A nothingness before birth, before the beginning of all things. This, perhaps, was the sound emitted by the cold white earth in the Ice Age.'

Snow is white. White—the colour of Galahad and the Holy Grail, of Oberon the Elf King, of polar bears and snow hares and owls and ermines. The snow-white trim of ermine fur on the robes of monarchs and emperors was once the symbol of justice, innocence and purity. 'As pure as the driven snow,' we say. Snowy-white is the apparel of the Angel of the Lord (Matthew), and of the resplendent Christ: 'And he was transfigured before them and his clothes became dazzling white, as white as snow' (Mark). Sufis see in snow the colour of wisdom, grace and transcendence, the colour of the light of the divine. 'In truth I am white,' said a lifelong devotee. 'I am a very old man, a sage whose essence is light.'

Snow is the curtain that conceals the mystery beyond this life. Under the shroud of snow all things vanish. Wrapped in its peaceful white blanket, one by one, we leave this world behind and travel to the next. Like waves washing over the sand, snow gently erases our footprints.

Snow symbolises not only the cold of death, but also the purity of Sünya, the void, the teeming abyss of infinite possibility, whose dazzling whiteness is devoid of all distinctions. In his last poem before death, the Zen monk Rippo welcomes the embrace of Sünya in the vision of snow.

> I have seen moon and blossoms; now I go
> to view the last and loveliest: the snow.

Named after the Sun Goddess, Fuchi Fujiyama, the 'Blue Rain' mountain is one of the most powerful symbols of Japanese culture and religion. A story from the distant past tells how the famous summit of Fuji came to be covered in snow. It begins when Mioya, ancestor of all the gods, decides to visit the world and see the sights. Mioya calls on Fuji expecting to be regally entertained and fed, but the ascetic Fuji refused to spend money on such frivolous niceties. Grossly offended, Mioya covered the mountain with eternal snow so that nothing would grow on its slopes. The idea was to discourage future visitors—it didn't work.

Instead, the snows of Fuji attract millions of pilgrims every year. They say that from its peak on a clear day you can see into heaven.

Snow is the ultimate expression of water's creative imaginings. Each snowflake is a gift, a work of art, yours for a fleeting second.

Snow begins its life when warm, moist air rises into a cold winter cloud. Carried by updraft winds the air vapour freezes, condensing into hexagonal ice crystals. As they descend, the crystals attract molecules of water vapour which attach themselves to the growing six-fold lattice in a symmetrical form. This is the act of creation, of water coming together with itself to produce divine art in the blue playground of the sky. And since divine art must express the endless creativity of the Divine Mind, no design will ever be the same.

Snow does not need clouds to form. In cold climates it can fall out of a clear blue sky. The fine crystals sparkling in the sunlight so dazzled polar explorers with their beauty, they were called 'diamond dust'.

Snowflakes vary in size. Some are big enough to frame and hang on your wall. I've heard of enthusiasts covering individual snowflakes with liquid superglue to create what they call 'fossilised' snow, solid permanent images that will not melt. It's a pity superglue wasn't invented in 1887; in January that year the largest snowflakes ever recorded fell across Fort Keogh in Montana. Measuring 38 centimetres (15 inches) in diameter, and 20 centimetres (8 inches) thick, they fell for miles around. A mail courier caught in the giant snowstorm verified the size of the flakes, but left no information about the impact of being hit by one. Did they fall gently? We will never know.

Another impressive snowfall occurred on the afternoon of 10 January 1915 in Berlin. 'Gigantic Snowflakes' read the newspaper headlines, eclipsing briefly news of the war that raged across Europe. The flakes, 8–10 centimetres (3–4 inches) in diameter, were not flat, but resembled round or oval dishes with the edges bent upwards.

A trillion crystal blossoms fall in every snowstorm, but who could count them? The weight of snow fallen since the earth began may be fifty times the mass of the planet, but that's not the most amazing thing. The most amazing thing is that out of all those billions upon billions of snowflakes, not one is the same. Not one.

The pattern of every snowflake is unique, but each comes in a hexagonal frame. Snowflakes offer us a kaleidoscope of visual imagery, a timeless source of intricate designs that have long inspired artists, poets, philosophers, and those who have eyes to see. The poet Hô-ô described them as 'delicate fretted hexagons of snow'.

Who sent these 'delicate fretted hexagrams'? By whom are they created? Just so you'll know, water personally signs each one. 'Flowers of plants and trees are generally five-pointed,' noted Han Ying in his journal (135 BC), 'but those of snow, which are called *Ying* are always six pointed.' To the scholar Tang Chin it seemed logical that 'since six is the number of water, when water congeals into flowers they must be six-pointed'.

Sixteen hundred years later Western scientific minds began to wonder why, from a Cartesian perspective, snowflakes had a consistent hexagonal form. The first European treatise to explore the repetitive geometrical perfection and multiplicity of pattern appeared in 1611. Its author was the mathematician and astronomer Johannes Kepler. 'Geometry existed before the creation of things,' Kepler asserted, 'as eternal as the spirit of God; it is God himself and gave him the proto-types for the creation of the world.'

One winter's day Kepler was out walking in search of inspiration when, he noted: 'by a happy chance water vapour was condensed into snow by the cold, and specks of down fell here and there on my coat, all with six corners and feathered radii'. Kepler set out to unravel the mystery, using the Socratic method. There must be a cause, he reasoned, because if it were by chance, then some flakes would have five corners and some seven. Why always six, he wondered.

Kepler came to the conclusion that the hexagonal shape of the snowflake, like the pentagonal shape of flowers and plants and the numerical constants, were all the work of a Supreme Intelligence. 'Snowflakes show us the Soul of the Earth', he wrote. Kepler published his reflections on snow geometry in a small leather-bound volume bearing the sub-title, 'On the Six Cornered Snowflake'. The 25-page essay was to form the basis for much future scientific conjecture.

After reading it, René Descartes published his detailed explanation of snow crystal structure, along with some drawings, in 1637. The first systematic study of snow crystals in 1681 was the work of Dowat Rosetti, an Italian priest and mathematician whose sixty sketches accompanied an essay on classification. Another contribution was the *Sekka Zusetsu*, 'Illustrations of Snow Blossoms', by the Japanese feudal lord, Toshitsura Ōinokami Doi, published in 1832. Using a compound microscope for his research, Doi added another 11 sketches to his second edition in 1839.

While debate continues about the cause of the sixfold symmetry of snow, the infinite variety of design was revealed by a Vermont farmer, W.A. Bentley. His lifelong love affair with snow began as a child when he was given a microscope by his mother. At first, Bentley drew the patterns that he saw through the lense, but this was frustrating because snowflakes don't last long. In 1885, when he was twenty, Bentley's parents bought him a bellows camera that could be attached to the microscope. With this apparatus, Bentley produced the first microphotographs of ice crystals.

For forty years he worked in his dairy, while continuing his research, producing four thousand images, two thousand of which were published in a book aptly titled *Snow Crystals* in 1931. It is still in print. Looking back on those years of interaction with snow, Bentley's enthusiasm remained undiminished. 'Under the microscope, I found that snowflakes were miracles of beauty,' he told an audience in 1925, 'and it seemed a shame that this beauty should not be seen and appreciated by others. Every crystal was a masterpiece of design and no design was ever repeated. When a snowflake melted, that design was forever lost. Just that much beauty was gone, without leaving any record behind.'

Could these images be a reflection of the mind of water? Are they the result of atmospheric conditions or can we see here the symbolic language of the Divine Intelligence?

You decide.

A factor that might influence your decision is a recent book by Dr Kenneth Libbrecht, a professor of physics in California. Illustrated by photographer

Patricia Rasmussen, *The Snowflake: Winter's Secret Beauty*, contains, according to one reviewer, 'the best snowflake images ever published'. Another volume for enthusiasts is *Snow Crystals* (1954) by the Japanese physicist, Ukichiro Nakaya. It contains 800 photographs which confirm once more the unique individuality of snowflake patterns. Nakaya called them 'hieroglyphs from heaven'.

A paper on the subject by Nittman and Stanly in 1987 begins: 'There is no answer to even the simplest of questions that one can pose about snowflake growth, such as why the six arms are roughly identical in length and why the overall pattern of each arm resembles the five others.' Could the answer lie outside the scientific paradigm?

'Where does snow come from?' I asked my grandfather one Christmas. My family were not big on boring scientific explanations. Instead, Alf told me the story of the Teutonic Goddess Holda, the White Woman who holds summer captive in her underground kingdom during winter. When Holda shakes out her bedclothes, snow falls. I remembered this story years later when I had my first experience of snow.

Living in an attic in an old house overlooking Hobart, I woke one morning to the unfamiliar sound of complete and utter silence. It was almost as if I had lost my hearing overnight. No birds, no cars, nothing.

I went to the window and looked out. The world was white and the sky was filled with white feathers drifting silently past, as if the Earth were dreaming. It brought back all those childhood memories of Christmas and Santa and sleighs and reindeer, of scorching hot summer days spent around artificial snow-laden pines in the living room. 'Santa Snow' came in aerosol cans. We sprayed it everywhere. Until I was 35, it was the only snow I had ever seen.

It's difficult for those of us who live in temperate climates to imagine the splendour of vast snowscapes. I envied Alexandra David-Neel her moonlight reveries among the glaciers of Tibet. 'Maybe elves of the frozen waterfalls, fairies of the snow and djinn-keepers of mysterious caves were to assemble and play and feast on the illuminated white tableland,' she wrote of one experience, 'or perhaps some grave council was to take place between the giants whose heads wore helmets of cold radiance.'

Who are the spirit 'fairies of the snow'? One appeared long ago to Sacred Otter, a Blackfoot warrior. Caught in a sudden blizzard while hunting buffalo on the open plains, Sacred Otter and his son made themselves a makeshift teepee out of fresh buffalo hide. Beneath it, insulated by the snow, they sank into a comfortable drowse induced by the gentle warmth.

Sacred Otter dreamed he was in the midst of a snow-covered landscape. Before him was a great white teepee crowned with golden light and painted with stars and symbols. While Sacred Otter circled the teepee admiring the art work he heard a deep voice say, 'Who walks around my teepee? Come in, come in!' He entered. The occupant, dressed in white, was smoking a black stone pipe. Sacred Otter sat before him.

For a long time they sat in silence, then the being spoke: 'I am Es-tonea-pesta, the Lord of Cold Weather and this snow teepee is my dwelling. I control the driving snow and the biting winds. You are here because I have taken pity on you and your son. Take the vision of this snow teepee with its symbols and medicines. Take also this mink-skin tobacco pouch, this black stone pipe and my supernatural power. You must build a teepee like this when you return to your camp!'

When Sacred Otter woke, the storm was over and he and his son made their way back to camp. Sacred Otter did as he was instructed and became a powerful shaman. Once more, while hunting buffalo, he and his companions were caught in another blizzard of epic proportions. This time Sacred Otter took out the black stone pipe, filled it with tobacco from the mink pouch and began to smoke. He blew the smoke in the direction of the storm and sang prayers to the Lord of Cold to have pity on his people. The storm abated long enough for everyone to get home safely, and the power of Sacred Otter's vision was confirmed.

Dreams of snow and their miraculous aftermath are not confined to shamanistic cultures. In 352 AD, a vision of the Virgin Mary appeared to a wealthy, childless Roman couple desperate to conceive. She told them that she wanted to have a church built in her honour in Rome. She would identify the desired site by covering it with snow. It was a busy night for Mary. She also called in on Pope Liberius who dreamed the same vision.

Next day, although it was warm, Rome awoke to find a floor plan of snow on the Esquilline Hill. The summer snowfall was proclaimed a genuine miracle, so the couple dedicated their wealth to the building of a church. Today on that same site stands the Basilica of St Mary Major, the seat of Our Lady of the Snows, where countless infertile couples come to pray.

Snowflakes and conception have a long association.

One of the many fables of Aesop tells of a woman whose husband was infertile. Having become pregnant by her more virile younger lover, she goes on a long journey. When she returns, she tells her husband that she conceived from a snowflake. The husband waited till the child was three, then he took the boy on a journey down to the warmer south. He returned alone, telling his wife that the snow child had melted in the hot sun.

Snowmen were originally religious images of deities associated with winter. Their creation was attended to with much ceremony and ritual. And eventually stories came into being about snowmen and women becoming animated and participating in the real world. One such legend is that of the Snowman Husband.

Among the Algonquin Indians there was once a woman of such exquisite beauty that she was called 'Handsome' (or its more eloquent Algonquin equivalent). One of her suitors, named 'Elegant' because of his rich costume and noble bearing, was rejected by Handsome both privately and publicly. Hurt and humiliated he became ill and depressed and refused to accompany his people on their winter migration to the warm plains of the south.

When everyone had gone, Elegant asked his guardian spirit to help him recover his dignity. Inspiration came. From the abandoned lodges, Elegant collected a pile of discarded clothing and rags. Making an armature of animal bones and cloth, he moulded the snow that had begun to fall into a tall imposing creature, ornamented with beads and brightly coloured feathers. Then with the power given him by his guardian, Elegant breathed life into his creation, naming the snowman Moowis.

The pair set out to catch up with the others and when they did, Moowis was a great social success. Even the chief entertained him as an honoured guest. Women vied for the attention of the noble stranger, none more than Handsome, and it was not long before the two were married.

Next day Moowis announced that he had to go on a journey to tell his people the good news. Handsome wanted to go with Moowis, but it was a long way he said, and dangerous. Finally she overcame his resistance and the two set out. The path led into cold mountains, through dense forests and across rocky valleys. Handsome was almost at the end of her tether when they descended once more to the plains where the heat of the sun revived her flagging spirits. At first Moowis tried to travel in the shade, but as the air became warmer he slowly dissolved and fell to pieces. All that remained was a pile of bones and rags and beads and feathers.

It is said that Handsome died of a broken heart, mourning the illusion she had loved so much. Indian people tell this parable around the fire on winter nights. When a man shows by his actions that he is more shadow than substance, more talk than action, they say he is like a snow-husband who vanishes when things heat up.

The newspapers of the 1950s and sixties often carried front-page stories of another creature of the snows—the Yeti—or, as the Western tabloids preferred to call him, the Abominable Snowman. Intrepid mountaineers returning from expeditions into the Himalayas brought photographs of giant footprints in the snow and stories of encounters with white furry ape-like creatures. Respected journals like *Science*, *Nature* and *New Scientist* explored theories and conjectures, including the possibility that the Yeti 'may be no other than the giant ape *Gigantopithecus blacki* persisting as a relic of the Pleistocene epoch in the seclusion of the Himalayas'.

In 1970, the British mountaineer Don Whillans got a clear view of a Yeti as it loped across the deep snow-covered slope of Mount Annapurna clutching a bag of Cadburys milk chocolates stolen from the expedition's tent. It was a big boost for the chocolate industry. In spite of all of these sightings no photos of Yetis have come to light, but the creature lives on in the folktales and legends of Tibet and Nepal, where as recently as 1958, the Yeti was listed as an officially protected species. There are reports of Yeti skulls preserved in monasteries as sacred relics, but none have been verified.

Yet another mystery of the snow remains unsolved. But still the most wonderful mystery is the possibility that in these fragile white flakes we may catch a brief glimpse of the mind of their Creator. 'How full of the creative genius is the air in which these are generated?' asks Henry Thoreau in 1856. 'I could hardly admire more if real stars fell and lodged on my coat.'

Nor could I, Henry, nor could I.

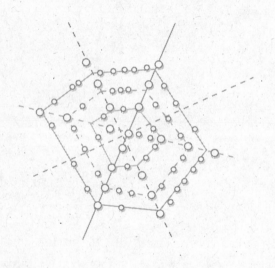

# The World of Dew

The spirit of the dew has its dwelling at the end
of the heavens and is connected with the
chambers of the rain, and its course is in the winter
and summer; and its clouds and the clouds of the
mist are connected, and the one passes over into
the other.

The Book of Enoch

My first taste of dew was spontaneous and unpre-meditated.

On an early morning climb to view the sunrise from a vantage point high in the Glasshouse Mountains, I came across a grove of mature grass trees in bloom. The flowers, flowing with dew and nectar, had already attracted a few early workers from the native bee community.

The grass tree, or *Xanthorrhoea*, is a bizarre plant. Its spear-shaped flower spike points upwards for 2 or 3 metres (6 to 9 feet) out of the centre of a skirt of brittle grass-like fronds growing on top of a thick black stem. Hundreds of small white flowers cover the bright green spike. Many bush specimens are at least 300 or 400 years old; some have survived for a thousand years.

I had heard that Aborigines soak the fresh flowers in water and drink the elixir that results. So, reaching up, I pulled down one of the massive stalks, closed my hand firmly around the base and drew it slowly up to the tip of the flower spike. There, pooled at the top of my closed fist, was a mouthful of dew. It was deli-cious—sweet–scented and aromatic. I repeated the process with several other plants. It was the most extraordinary breakfast I have ever had. The rising sun found me still at work feasting on the nectar of heaven.

Such was my initiation into the world of dew.

Of all the manifestations of water, dew is the one most laden with symbolic significance. Dew is simultaneously the nectar of the Rosicrucians, the philosopher's mercury, astral rain, the liquid essence of the Divine, the Green Lion, the elixir of immortality drunk by pharaohs and emperors seeking to enhance (and extend) their connection with the cosmic energy of the Universe.

Maori people see dew as tears shed by the Sky God for his lost love. The Sky Father Rangi and his consort Papa (Mother Earth) had to be parted so that life could begin in the intervening space between them. Though they remain forever separated, their love for one another is expressed every day as Papa's soft warm sighs of longing ascend to heaven from the forested mountains and plains. Humans call these 'mists'. And Rangi, as he mourns through the long lonely nights of eternal separation, weeps profusely. His tears fall on Papa's breasts and the green valleys of her body, and humans seeing his tears call them dew drops.

It's difficult to believe that this is the same dew that silently moistens our lawns and gardens under cover of darkness, sparkling like diamonds in the early morning sun.

As a child I was fascinated by the heavy falls of dew that covered our thick buffalo grass lawn, and dripped steadily from the leaves of the massive mulberry tree outside my bedroom window onto the galvanisèd iron roof. One day I asked Alfred, my maternal grandfather, where dew came from. Alf was my authority on all things magical. He had answers for any question no matter how strange or obscure. 'Dew,' said Alf, in a serious voice, 'is made by fairies who work at night by the light of the moon, bringing jugs of nectar to sprinkle on the grass and plants in order to nourish the land'.

Years later I discovered that Alf's theory about the supernatural origins of dew was shared by indigenous healers, Old Testament prophets, ancient Egyptian priests and Chinese alchemists. Oshadegea, the Great Dew Eagle of the Iriquois whose lodge is in the western sky, carries a lake of dew in the middle of his back.

Just as the combination of sun and rain produces rainbows, so dew creates dewbows, displaying the seven colours of the spectrum. These are more frequent in autumn when hundreds of tiny spider webs, spun between blades of grass, hold dewdrops suspended above the ground. Ashanti Demiurge, the spider deity of the Bambara, an east African tribe, first created the sun, moon and stars, and divided night from day. Then she created dew. Dew is what spiders drink. If you take the time to study larger webs spun between trees, you can watch spiders in the early morning quenching their thirst with the nectar of the gods.

Another strange optical effect to look for on dew-covered fields or lawns is the *heiligenschein*. If you stand so that your elongated shadow is projected onto the ground by the rising sun, a halo of light will appear around your head—the blessing of the dew. This may be as near as you'll ever get to sainthood! 'An aureole of glory has rested on my head,' wrote the sixteenth-century sculptor Benvenuto Cellini, believing that God had recognised his talent. 'This is visible,' he continued, 'to every sort of man to whom I have chosen to point it out.'

For centuries, learned folk believed that pearls were formed from drops of dew. A Spanish Rabbi, Benjamin of Tudela, travelling in Persia in 1173 observed that, 'In these places pearls are found, made by the wonderful artifice of nature: for on the four and twentieth day of the month Nisan, a certain dew falleth into the waters which being sucked in by the oysters, they immediately sink to the bottom of the sea'. The theory of dew-formed pearls was embraced by the pioneer English naturalist, William Camden (1551–1623), who stated that 'the shell fish eagerly sucking in the dew, conceive and bring forth pearls or shell berries'.

The concept of dew as a magical substance has long appealed to the popular imagination. One of the most enduring beliefs is that washing your face with dew will do wonders for your skin. In the northern hemisphere the energy of dew is reputed to reach its peak during the month of May. In 1791, a London newspaper reported that, 'yesterday, being the first of May, a number of persons went into the fields and bathed their faces with the dew on the grass with the idea that it would render them beautiful'.

And, when you think about it, why stop there? Among the native peoples of British Columbia the custom of rolling naked in the dew-laden grass was part of an initiation ceremony aimed at acquiring a guardian spirit. In Russia it was thought to enhance the productivity of the land if a priest rolled across the newly-sown fields. Whether naked or clothed was not recorded. In nineteenth century Holland, 'dew-treading' was the term used to describe lovemaking in the morning dew as a re-enactment of the fertility rituals of earlier times.

I, too, have made love in the dew at the rising of the sun. I think that by participating in the traditions and beliefs of the past we can explore their meaning and potency, and plumb their hidden depths. Making love among dew diamonds is an unforgettable experience.

Dew formed the basis of many antique magic spells and potions. *Spiritus Universalis* is a mixture of equal parts of dew, rainwater and melted snow which enabled its maker to take a remnant of anything and view it whole in its original form. For instance, 'He can sprinkle the ashes of a plant with it and . . . even if the plant has been dead for thousands of years, he will see it as it once was'.

Dew was an essential ingredient in the recipes of medieval alchemists, the founding fathers of the modern science of chemistry. In their quest for the elusive Philosophers Stone—which would transmute the base metal of everyday existence into the gold of mystical illumination—alchemists were obsessed with the phenomena of chemical change. For them, dew was the primal celestial fluid, pregnant with magic potential, the *materia prima* from which all other matter is created.

One alchemical text, the *Mutus Liber*—the 'Wordless Book'—contains 15 graphic allegorical engravings, a series of snapshots of the process used to collect dew and distil its essence. Page four shows dew being collected on calico sheets spread out on wooden stands. In the morning the sheets are wrung out over a wide dish providing an ample quantity of the precious liquid. The anonymous seventeenth-century author claimed to have been inspired by biblical references, which celebrate the spiritual and material qualities of dew. Isaiah, for example, compares the healing power of dew gathered from herbs to the Dew of the Resurrection, said to be stored in *Arabot*, the highest heaven. This gift of the Holy Spirit could restore life to the lifeless and revitalise parched souls. The Psalms contain another intriguing passage that attracted the attention of alchemists and provided the name for the Estée Lauder perfume, Youth Dew. 'From the womb of the morning, you will receive the dew of your youth.' This reference to 'the womb of the morning' connects with Egyptian scriptures, which describe dew as the vaginal fluid of Tefnut, the Goddess of Moisture. Tefnut was depicted as a serpent wound around the pharaoh's sceptre, indicating that as long as she supported his reign there would never be drought. Christian mystics even went so far as to asso-ciate dew with the impregnating fluid of God himself.

The speedy evaporation of dew is a reminder that life is transient and brief. It's a powerful metaphor for philosophers and poets wishing to emphasise the ephemeral nature of existence. 'Your love is like a morning mist,' sings Hosea rebuking the people of Israel for straying from the paths of righteousness, 'like the early dew that disappears.' In the Japanese haiku, *The World of Dew*, the Zen monk Issa (1763–1827) mourns the untimely death of his young daughter.

Although he knows that the material world is only an illusion, grief and loss still seem only too real.

> Dew evaporates
> and all our world
> is dew . . . So dear,
> so refreshing, so fleeting . . .

The London physician Dr W.C. Wells published *A Theory of Dew* in 1814 inspired by a passage in the Old Testament where Gideon asks God to indicate his existence by inundating a wool fleece with dew while leaving the surrounding ground dry. Next day Gideon wrings out the fleece in front of the doubters and fills a bowl with dew. Then he asks God for another sign— to leave the fleece dry but cover the ground with dew. And, of course, so it was. Wells used sheepskins to demonstrate that dew falls only on surfaces that are exposed to the sky. From this he deduced that dew must come down from the heavens and not up from the earth, as many had supposed.

Today's scientific explanation goes something like this: On cool clear nights not cold enough to produce frost, moisture in the air condenses to form globules. After sunset, when the warm vegetation radiates its heat back into space, plants and grass cool rapidly until their surface temperature is lower than that of the surrounding air and a thin layer of moisture is deposited on leaves, flowers and any surface exposed to the sky.

If the sky is cloudy, the temperature balance between earth and atmosphere is maintained and radiation does not disperse. Under these conditions there will be less condensation whereas in cloudless regions where there is little rainfall, more dew will be deposited.

In arid areas, the annual dewfall provides essential moisture to plant and animal life. The deserts of Turkey, Israel and other Middle Eastern countries have remnants of 3000-year-old mounds of stones and pebbles that condense moisture from the atmosphere so that it seeps down to irrigate the earth below. In the centre of these mounds fig and olive trees thrive. This technique, coupled with an intimate understanding of dew gained through centuries of observation and experimentation, enabled desert farmers to survive and prosper.

Dew that falls in rainforests is a different story altogether. Have you ever wondered about the origin of the term 'rainforest'? It was used by explorers to describe the remarkable cycle of moisture movement that takes place beneath the thick canopy. In 1851 Alexander von Humbolt observed: 'In the South American forests, notwithstanding the sky is perfectly clear overhead, rain frequently falls in heavy showers, caused by the copious formation of dew by the radiating powers of the tops of the trees in contact with the vapour-laden atmosphere of the tropics.'

According to Chinese myth the Tree of Sweet Dew is situated at the centre of the world on Mount Kun Lun. Its liquid confers the gift of eternal life on those who consume it regularly. Coincidentally, the Jewish *Kabbalah* envisages dew as the mystical emanation of the Tree of Life.

The myth of the Tree of Sweet Dew, like many such stories, has its origin in nature. The Traveller's Tree on the island of Madagascar is one example. The trunk terminates in a cluster of three metre (ten feet) long broad leaves whose stalks embrace the tree in sheaths that catch and retain the dew, forming reservoirs of cool refreshing water.

The Rain Tree of the Canary Islands is another natural water provider. In his seventeenth-century account of the conquest of the Canaries, the Spanish historian Juan de Abreu Galindo described an enormous laurel tree which was the sole source of drinking water for the inhabitants of the island of Ferro. This vegetable fountain was enveloped in morning cloud and the water that dripped from it was collected and poured into cisterns. The existence of the sacred tree was revealed to the invading Spaniards by a courtesan who paid with her life for her treachery.

In fact, there is not one Rain Tree in the Canaries but a valley of them; this is the world's oldest rain-forest. At the Parque Nacional de Garajonay of the Isle of La Gomera is a forest of massive laurels that have survived since the last Ice Age. The continuously dripping trees sit in puddles of their own moisture, part dew and part swirling mist. No-one collects it any more. The locals now drink chlorinated water from their taps.

They don't know what they're missing.

The liquid that pools beneath Rain Trees and flows from the leaves of Traveller's Trees is not the result of condensation. It comes from deep down beneath the earth, drawn up through the living tissues of the host plant before it emerges. Far more powerful than condensed dew, this fluid contains the essence of the plants and flowers that give it birth. Alchemists call it 'sparkling dew' to distinguish its properties from those of 'virgin dew', produced by condensation. Macro photography reveals that each drop of 'sparkling dew' displays the same range of the colour spectrum as that of a rainbow. It is, I suggest, 'sparkling dew' that creates the dewbows that glitter in the early morning sunlight.

The scientific term for 'sparkling dew' is guttation, derived from the word 'gutter'. Robbed of its mystery, guttation is explained as just another simple mechanical process. 'All plants transport large quantities of water from their roots to their leaves where it evaporates. When the air is humid although the water transport continues, the water vapour cannot evaporate into air, which is already saturated. The water is exuded as droplets from the tips of leaves and grass.' No matter what you call it, 'sparkling dew', even when mingled with 'virgin dew', appears to possess healing properties.

Early medical experiments with dew began with alchemy. Paracelsus collected dew on angled sheets of glass under various astrological configurations in the hope that if the energy of the stars could be transferred to the dew, then it might have a useful healing function.

Three hundred years later in the 1930s, Edward Bach, an eminent surgeon, pathologist and bacteriologist, abandoned his practice in London's fashionable Harley Street and retreated to an isolated Welsh village. Depressed by the failure of modern 'scientific' medicine to provide an adequate response to illness and disease, Bach turned to nature for inspiration.

One May morning, walking through fields wet with dew, it occurred to him that every dewdrop must extract some of the properties of the plant on which it rested. The heat of the sun, magnified through the fluid, would further enhance these energies, magnetising every drop with power. If it were possible, he thought, to collect this uncontaminated essence it would be an ideal medium for homeopathic medicines. Testing the effects of dew from various plants and flowers on himself and his patients, Bach evolved the system of herbal remedies that bears his name. It remains in popular use today.

Some of Bach's flower essences were developed to treat agitation, anger, sorrow and distress. Flower tinctures and infusions fulfil a similar function in traditional Chinese medicine. Chrysanthemums for instance, were prescribed, with dew if possible, as an antidote to depression. Poet Tao Yuan Ming wrote:

> Autumn chrysanthemums have a lovely tint,
> I pluck their fresh petals so full of dew.
> Drowned in this sorrow-banishing liquor
> I leave behind a world-laden heart.
> Though I enjoy the goblet all alone . . .

Chrysanthemums, dew and banishment figure in the story of Keu Tze Tung, who unintentionally offended the Emperor Hu Wang. Banished from the palace in disgrace, the courtier fled to the Valley of Chrysanthemums where he lived on dew collected from the flowers and eventually achieved immortality. In a Buddhist version, Keu Tze possessed a magic text which, when painted on the chrysanthemum petals, enhanced the potency of the dew.

Dew was the diet of choice for those Chinese obsessed with extending their life span. According to Lao Tzu, the elite Immortals who occupied the prime real estate on the Isle of the Blessed lived on nothing else. Emperors who aspired to join them incorporated dew into their early morning rituals. 'Pure dew', wrote one, 'collected without contamination with earthly things confers the enviable blessing of immortality on the fortunate being who is successful at quenching his thirst at the dawn of day with a precious draught.' The Han Emperor We drank his precious draught spiced with finely powdered jade, served in a carved jade chalice.

The conspicuous consumption of dew was not just about attaining immortality. There were other important symbolic significances. In Chinese tradition, dew is associated with the princely power of yang as opposed to the yin energy of rain. The fall of dew is a sign of the peaceful marriage of heaven and earth. By consuming it, the Emperor participated in this process. The Emperor Wu Ti, anxious to prolong his life, had a tall tower built in the palace garden. On its summit was a large bronze image of an Immortal holding a wide-mouthed golden vase in which dew collected.

However, you don't need to go to such extremes. In his book, *The Gold of a Thousand Mornings*, the modern French alchemist Armand Barbault points out that far more dew can be gathered by dragging linen sheets along the ground, across the tops of plants or grasses. The qualities and properties of this will, of course, depend on the plants from which it is collected.

There are many ways to connect with this gift from heaven. You can drink it, bathe in it, walk barefoot through it, suck it directly from flowers or make love in it if the spirit so moves you.

The Balinese believe that after cremation has dispersed the remains of the material body into the air, the soul returns to earth in the dew. If you lie face down on the ground in the early morning, you will see each blade of grass holding a precious drop on its point, millions of returned souls, all glittering in the sun!

# THE
# WATERS
# BELOW

# The Mysteries of the Ice

The Ice adds by removing, transforms without creating, informs by obscuring. It's meaning does not reside within...awaiting revelation but derives from the illumination brought to it from outside. Ice does not merely reflect mind; it absorbs it. The more it absorbs the larger it becomes; the more light brought to it, the more powerful its reflection.

Stephen J. Pyne
*The Ice*

Beautiful, enchanting and dangerous, ice is water's solid incarnation. But all ice is not equal. The iceblocks in your freezer made from tap water are 'tame' ice, domesticated and controlled. This is the ice with which most of us are familiar. The ice that forms in winter on the surface of lakes and ponds is frozen water, too, but of a higher order. But there's yet another kind of ice—wild ice—made not from frozen water but from compressed snowflakes and ice crystals laid down layer upon layer since the last great age when ice ruled the world.

As the Earth warmed, the wild ice gradually retreated to the glacial peaks of high mountain ranges and the North and South poles. While the Arctic regions support human populations, which have adapted and learned to co-exist with ice, Antarctica has no history of human occupation, no stories, no myths. Yet, beneath its white landscape lies the recorded history of the Earth's climate for uncounted millennia. Each crystal carries information about the state of the climate at the time it was laid down. This ice is the memory bank of the planet.

In *Journey to the Centre of the Earth*, Jules Verne's nineteenth-century science-fiction novel, his heroes discover a vast lake far below the surface. Now, with the help of modern sonar equipment scientists have discovered that Verne's fantasy is a reality. Four kilometres (2.5 miles) under the ice lies a huge freshwater lake 200 kilometres long (125 miles) and 700 metres (765 yards) deep. And it is just one of several. How could this water remain unfrozen with millions of tonnes of ice on top of it? Is this where the heat from the molten core of the Earth meets the frozen ice above? What marvellous stories could this water tell us? There are other spiritual and esoteric dimensions beyond the scientific perspective of Antarctica.

Since water is immortal we should not be surprised when it confounds the relatively recent man-made 'laws' of science. The behaviour of ice contradicts a fundamental principle of physics, which states that the density of matter increases as it moves from gas to liquid to solid. When water freezes, it reverts to its crystal state, forming cavities that fill with air, decreasing its density and allowing it to float on the mother liquid. That's why an iceblock floats in a glass of water. When it does so, you are witnessing a miracle of nature. If that iceblock were to sink, so would the rest of the world's ice and before long the oceans, lakes and rivers of the world would freeze from the bottom up. A new Ice Age would begin, one that none of us would survive.

But then again, some of us might. In Tibet, *thumo reskiang*, the ability to demonstrate one's resistance to extreme cold is a religious discipline. After months of instruction, disciples undergo a final test. Sitting by a frozen lake or river they must dry, with the heat of their bodies, several sheets dripping with icy water. Once initiated they spend days and nights, sitting naked and motionless among the snow and whirling winter blizzards.

You don't have to travel to remote glaciers or polar regions to find wild ice. Vestiges of past ice ages remain, concealed beneath the Earth in unexpected places, such as New Mexico, Argentina, Hawaii, Hungary and the Canary Islands. Below the surface of the deserts of south-western USA, for example, lie huge subterranean grottos packed with ice of unknown origin and unfathomable depth. The ice cave on the Candelaria Ranch in Valencia County, New Mexico, is a typical example. Six metres (20 feet) down, but fully exposed to the temperature of the outside air, the cave's contents reveal themselves. None know the age of its glass-like aquamarine walls. Worshipped as a sacred place by indigenous people since prehistoric times, the cave was a godsend (so to speak) to the first white settlers in this hot region. They carted the primeval ice away in wagonloads to refrigerate food and replenish their drinking water supplies. The store of ice seems to be inexhaustible.

Another 'natural refrigerator' can be found 3000 metres (almost 1000 feet) above sea level on the 'Peak of Teneriffe' in the Canary Islands. 'The cave supplies the ice consumed in these islands,' writes William Corliss, 'from which it may be inferred that the quantity is not insignificant.' Reputed to possess healing powers, the ice is widely used as a medicine. It too has never been known to fail.

Ice is the source of many great rivers, which originate in high mountain glaciers, themselves slow moving rivers of ice. These remnants of the last Ice Age are constantly melting, continuously replenished by snow falling on their peaks. The Gangotri glacier is revered by millions. Here Mother Ganges makes her dramatic entry into the world, pouring out of a sacred ice cave known as 'The Cow's Mouth'. Holy men dressed in little more than loincloths spend months at a time meditating, bathing in the freezing water and drinking from the fast-running stream.

In its most powerful incarnation—in the remote windswept peaks of the Himalayas or the white, impenetrable silence of Antarctica—ice generates a mixture of respect, fear, and awe in those who venture into her realm. The quest to 'conquer' Everest or to plant some national flag at the North and South Poles is a chronicle of danger, disaster and death. Even those who have been successful have had to hastily retreat after a few brief moments of triumph. The unfamiliar white landscape with its bizarre lightshows and weird other-worldly sculptural forms plays strange tricks on the mind, while sudden death from blizzards, avalanches and treacherous hidden crevasses is never far away.

Preparing for his 1928 Antarctic Expedition, Admiral Richard E. Byrd included two coffins and twelve strait jackets in his list of essentials. He had been there before. Not for nothing did H.P. Lovecraft call his disturbing fantasy of the ancient polar under-world, *At the Mountains of Madness*. 'The outer world of icy desolation has also descended on the inner world of our souls,' lamented Frederick Cook in the grip of the dreaded Antarctic white night. The white night, or whiteout as it's sometimes called, occurs when sun-illuminated clouds produce a brilliant light, which is reflected and intensified by the myriad prismatic mirrors of the ice. Visibility vanishes, shadows disappear, the horizon is lost and contrast becomes instead a milky trembling nothingness which confuses consciousness and convolutes rational thought. 'Space, time and the presence of an other against which one can define self all dissolve' writes Stephen Pyne. 'The observer is left with literally nothing to observe. Art and science, mind and sight, require contrast: without some darkness there is no meaning to daylight. Instead, the whiteout produces a sweet light, an unpleasant mysticism that illuminates everything and enlightens nothing'.

Another factor that disturbs the psychic balance of humans is the coloured lighting. They must endure twenty-four hour days of blue and green skies. The only contrast comes in the evening twilight when white ice becomes dark purple and the sky turns lemon green.

The journals of polar travellers and the myths of the indigenous peoples of the Arctic tell many stories of strange images in the sky. Shamans say that the water is dreaming. And what dreams they are. Mirages appear as frequently in seascapes, ice fields and cold climates as they do in hot dry deserts.

In *South*, Ernest Shackleton's story of his 1914 expedition to Antarctica, he tells of 'a wonderful mirage of the Fata Morgana type . . . great white and golden cities of Oriental appearance . . . floating above these are wavering violet and creamy lines . . . everything wears an aspect of unreality'. The Fata Morgana is named after a magical city beneath the sea created by the Arthurian enchantress Morgan le Fay to lure sailors to their deaths. Friar Antonio Minasi had three separate encounters in the Straits of Messina in Italy for which, being a good Dominican, he attempts to find a rational explanation.

His 1773 description is intriguing. With his back to the sun and his face to the sea, Minasi 'sees appear in the water, as in a catoptric theatre, various multiplied objects such as numberless series of pilasters, arches, castles well delineated, regular columns, lofty towers, superb palaces with balconies and windows, extended alleys of trees, delightful plains with herds and flocks, armies of men on foot and horseback, and many other strange figures, all in their natural colours and proper action, and passing rapidly in succession along the surface of the sea, during the whole short period of time . . .'. Would a Dominican monk make all this up? Maybe water does dream after all.

On 26 January 1901, *The Victoria Daily Times* of British Columbia published a photograph taken in 1887 of a mirage that appeared every year for centuries, above the ice of the Muir glacier. Known as 'the silent city of Alaska', it could be seen between the hours of 7 and 9 am any day from June 21 to July 10. To the local Indians who had been observing it for generations, it was a vision of the Afterlife. Some more travelled observers compared it to an ancient city of the past while others thought that it rather resembled the English city of Bristol.

The fantastic sculptured forms of wild ice express the boundless creative imagination of water in every curve and pinnacle. Just as river, glacier and ocean carve the Earth, so water is constantly forming and reforming both itself and the world around us.

Ice is a magnificent medium for artists and sculptors, though often neglected because of its ephemeral nature. While inspired Oriental chefs create magnificent ice swans and dragons and crystal bowls as decorative utilitarian centrepieces for banquets in a tradition that's thousands of years old, modern ice sculpture is now a widely recognised art form. The exhibitions at the Chinese *Ice and Snow Festival* (Harbin, 31 December) and the Sapporo Snow Festival (Hokkaido, Japan, February) provide an opportunity for ice sculptors to exhibit to international audiences.

Ice is also a versatile and speedy building material. Although the indigenous domed igloos of the Alaskan Inuit are perhaps its most famous example, grand and imposing palaces of ice have long been a source of wonder and enchantment. How many of these great edifices have melted into history we will never know, but modern ice architecture seems to have its origin in Czarist Russia in a structure built beside the frozen River Neva in the winter of 1739 for the amusement of the Empress Anna Ivanova. Designed by the royal architect Europkin, the stylistic extravaganza of domes, spires and minarets, although modest in scale, drew hundreds of thousands of spectators.

A century later, Canadians began to build ice castles as part of their winter festivities. Some were truly magnificent fantasies of glowing ice with glittering lit interiors, glistening transparent walls, spacious halls and vast corridors. The St Pauls ice palace of 1885 was the most spectacular. Lost for words, journalists turned to extravagant metaphors seldom used to describe Victorian architecture. 'An enchanted castle . . . like the marvellous imaginings of some opium sated dream,' gushed a *New York Times* critic. A 'weird mystic palace of fairy fancy,' said another.

> There is a popular fallacy to the effect that the Ice Palace is built; built by mere men who saw out the blocks of ice with saws, heave them with ice-tongs and derricks into place and lay them as the commonplace bricklayer lays bricks. But this is all nonsense . . . Look at it! Look at the light vaulting arches and stately turrets. Massive it stands, but as light as a castle of clouds. Mysteriously beautiful and dim in its semi-translucency, and glittering from and thousand diamond facets where the winter sun strikes its angles. All the gods of Asgard never built anything more lovely. Alph, the sacred river, flowed by no structure more majestically fairy-like. That thing built by men? Nonsense! It rose as the walls of Athens rose, to the sound of the music of gods.

The reference to 'the music of gods' reminds us that ice has yet another dimension. It sings, continuously, a song older than the beginning of time. Wild ice has its own unique voice, one of water's many dialects.

Walking alone on the frozen surface of Lake Baikal under the light of the full moon, the Russian environmentalist Valentin Rasputin had an extraordinary experience:

> Baikal spread out wider and wider before me . . . I walked and walked . . . long shafts of thunder came running at me under the ice, exploding and rumbling directly beneath my feet but I quickly got used to them and stopped being afraid . . . It was as if I had entered some kind of enchanted kingdom of forces different from those we know, of different sounds and times that make up a different life . . . Baikal grumbled with a muffled sweetness, somewhere little ice bells tinkled in a strumming trickle, somewhere something flowed and subsided with a sigh.

In the spring of 2003, Peter Cusack travelled to Lake Baikal to record the songs and symphonies of the sacred lake. His CD is called *Baikal Ice*. Listen to it at night. Give yourself over to its eerie harmonies and, there in the darkness, you will hear what Rasputin heard, the voice of water singing through the ice.

# The Springs of Antiquity

By tall trees a century old,
I breathe the fragrance of a myriad ages,
I drink at the springs of antiquity...

Hsieh Ling Yun 385–433 AD

Ten thousand years ago a group of hunter-gatherers decided to settle beside a freshwater spring at a place called Jericho in what is now Israel. It was a pivotal moment in human history—agriculture, architecture, the ownership of land and dwelling, urban sprawl—this is where it all began. Each succeeding generation built on the ruins of the past, so that today we have a vertical record of ten thousand years of human settlement. It's called the Tell of Jericho. And, at the very bottom of the Tell of Jericho, archaeologists found not only the original mud brick village, but also the same spring used to supply their water, still flowing as pure as ever.

Welling up from deep within the earth, each spring carries the memory of its unique origins. Springs offer us an opportunity to make our own direct and personal connection with this living water, the mythic Water of Life. Little wonder, then, that the worship of springs is one of our most enduring rituals. Long before there were doctors, shamans, medicine men or healers, living water was the panacea for all ills. As cultures and religions evolved, their relationship with the sacred springs of their primal ancestors flowered into myths and stories, poetry and song.

Sitting under a tree beside the thousand-year-old spring of Tirta Empul in the mountains of Bali, I listened while Made Aka explained the significance of springs in Balinese cosmology. 'This world we see and experience,' he said, 'the visible phenomena that surrounds us, is the realm of Maya, the Goddess of Illusion. We inhabit an empty space between the polarities of the Gods who generate growth and fertility on the one hand and the demons who represent death and dissolution on the other. These two opposing forces created the Middle World as a stage where the eternal cycles of growth and decay, birth and death follow one another as surely as the moon follows the sun.' The Balinese envisage springs as magic portals, gateways to the spirit realm, where the veil of illusion that separates the middle from the other worlds may be lifted. Here spiritual energy may manifest itself in material form.

Near the village of Aorrangi in the Cook Islands, is the spring of Vaitipi. One night after the full moon when everyone was sleeping, a woman and man of dazzling white complexion rose up out of the crystal waters of Vaitipi. They came from the land of spirits deep below, to steal taro, bananas, plantains and coconuts. On one of these excursions the pair were seen by a restless insomniac walking near the spring. The clan devised a plan to catch the spirits. After the next full moon, the couple materialised and set off to pillage the plantations. While they were away a great net was spread at the bottom of the spring. Then the village raised the alarm, chasing the startled spirits back into the water. The female dived first and found herself trapped. The villagers carried her off in triumph while others reset the net but a small space remained uncovered and the male managed to escape.

The captive became the cherished wife of Ati, who filled the hole at the bottom of the pool with massive stones so that she could not return to her world. She was named Tapairu (the peerless one) for her beauty and wisdom. Tapairu became reconciled to the ways of mortals and eventually gave birth to a son. When the boy was weaned, Tapairu went to Ati and asked whether he would allow her to return to the nether regions. Finally he consented but only if he could accompany her. The clan removed the boulders and Tapairu collected vegetable gums from the forest and smeared these over Ati's body to ease his descent into the spirit world. Holding firmly on to Ati's hand, Tapairu dived with him into the clear depths of the pool. They tried several dives, but each time Ati ran out of breath and had to return to the surface. Only the immortals and the spirits of the dead may enter through such doorways. The weeping couple embraced for the last time, then Tapairu dived down and disappeared before the eyes of the people. She was never seen again.

The roots of Yggdrasil, the Cosmic World Tree of Scandinavia, draw sustenance from three magic springs. The first is Urdar, the Spring of Judgement where the gods dispense justice and determine the fate of the world. Keeping watch over Urdar are the Norns, personifications of the past, present and future. Every morning, the Norns draw water from Urdar to sprinkle on the branches of Yggdrasil; it falls to earth as honeydew.

The second spring fills the Well of Mimir (Memory), the fountain of wit and wisdom in whose liquid depths the future is clearly mirrored. In the morning of time the god Odin came to drink its waters and absorb their powers, but the guardian would accept nothing less than an eye as payment for one cup of the precious liquid. Such was his desire that Odin plucked out one of his eyes, laid it in the spring and drank the waters of knowledge, prophecy and poetry. The third spring is the Infernal Fountain, the seething cauldron of hell, home of the serpent Nidhug who feeds on the bones of the dead.

The association of water and memory as epitomised by the Well of Mimir is reflected in the Greek Muses, who were the daughters of Mnemosyne (Memory). The word 'memory' itself is derived from 'mem' the ancient Hebrew designation for water.

The nine Muses were performance artists. They sang at mythic parties, weddings and funerals and inspired poets, musicians and artists who invoked their presence and left offerings on their altars. The Springs of the Muses included Pierene at Corinth (Lais, acknowledged as the most beautiful courtesan of her generation was described as 'even more glittering than the clear waters of Pierene), the Castalian Spring on Mount Parnassus, and the Hippocrene on Mount Helicon. The last was the venue of an extraordinary competition with the Pierids, a choir of nine sisters who had the temerity to challenge the Muses' claim to fame. The Pierids gave a magnificent performance that the assembled gods applauded enthusiastically. Then came the Muses. According to eyewitness accounts, as the melody of their song reached its crescendo even the sea and stars stood enchanted, rivers withheld their flow and the mountain itself began to rise towards the heavens.

Poseidon was alarmed. Something had to be done to stop Mount Helicon's ascent. Calling Pegasus, the winged horse whose name means 'springs of water', Poseidon ordered him to stamp his hoof on the mountain peak. The rock was shattered by the impact and the Hippocrene spring burst forth. It was the greatest concert finale of them all. A French manuscript from the fourteenth century shows Pegasus striking with his hoof, while the spring flows down the mountain slope where it collects in a circular pool in which the nine nude Muses celebrate their victory.

The Spring of Salmacis in Greece had a unique reputation. It was said that whoever bathed there would lust after people of the same sex—and it all came about because of a nymph's prayer. Atlantides, the teenage son of Aphrodite and Hermes, was renowned for his handsome looks and elegant bearing. One of his most ardent admirers was the forest nymph, Salmacis. Ignoring the fact that Atlantides had only just turned fifteen, she made the boy an offer she thought he couldn't refuse. When he rejected her amorous advances, it made Salmancis more determined than ever. Secretly, she began to stalk the object of her unwanted affection.

Hiding behind a leafy shrub, the lusty nymph watched Atlantides undress and bathe in the crystal clear waters of a forest spring. Unable to contain herself, Salmacis tore off her flimsy tunic and jumped in with him. Clinging tightly to the startled lad she begged the gods to unite them forever. Her prayer was answered, but the outcome was not quite what she expected. Suddenly Atlantides and Salmacis literally became one person with both male and female attributes and genitalia. He/she took the title of Hermaphroditus, but the spring itself was named after Salmacis. It drew many devotees to bathe and drink its waters.

Greek springs were revered as sources of prophecy, healing, magic and divination. Each had its own guardian in the form of a female nymph or Naiade whose presence was invoked by those who came to seek the water's blessing. The Naiades were virgins, their purity and spirituality equated with sexual abstinence. But keeping one's virginity among the highly-sexed gods and satyrs of Greek mythology seems to have been a constant struggle.

The nymph Castalia, pursued by Apollo, transformed herself into a spring at Delphi on Mount Parnassus, one that communicated through a priestess known as the Pythia. Water flowed from the Castalian spring through seven bronze lions' mouths into a marble basin in which the Pythia bathed. Prophecy was thought of as a divine madness. Drinking the water of the spring filled the Pythia temporarily with its powers, and through her, the water spoke.

Another water nymph who fought to retain her virtue was Arethusa. In his *Metamorphoses*, Ovid tells how, worn out from a hard day's hunting in the forest, Arethusa came to a stream that flowed: 'So clear I could see right to the bottom, and count every pebble in its depths. You would scarcely have thought that it was moving at all. Silver willows and poplars drawing nourishment from the water, spread natural shade over its sloping banks. I went up and dipped my feet in the stream, and then my legs, up to the knees. Not content with that, I unfastened my girdle, hung my soft garments on a drooping willow, and plunged naked into the waters. As I swam with a thousand twists and turns striking the water and drawing it towards me, threshing my arms about, I felt a kind of murmuring in the midst of the pool and, growing frightened, leapt onto the nearer bank . . .'

It was a wise move. Alpheius, the river god, was filled with such desire for Arethusa that he pursued the nymph relentlessly. When she fled into the forest he transformed himself into a hunter. There seemed to be no escape. Desperate, Arethusa invoked the assistance of the goddess Artemis who changed her into a spring. Alpheius immediately reverted to his river incarnation so that he could mingle his waters with hers. This was frustrated by Artemis who sent the fugitive spring, via a cavern under the sea bed, to the island of Ortygia off the coast of Syracuse where Arethusa finally burst forth and flowed down to the sea. Undaunted, the ardent Alpheius crossed the Adriatic as a freshwater current before finally uniting with the object of his desire. There in the fogbound plain of the sea their continuous consummation is daily re-enacted as the foaming mouth of Alpheius mingles with the gushing spring of Arethusa.

This extraordinary spring still flows on Ortygia, the oldest part of the city of Syracuse, its circular pond ringed with papyrus. This is the only place outside

Egypt where papyrus grows naturally. Arethusa was elevated to the status of a divinity. Her image, surrounded by dolphins, appears on many Syracusan coins.

Many freshwater springs well up from the ocean floor, reaching the surface of the sea with a fountain-like dome. People living in the Greek Islands used to row out to swim in their pristine water and take barrels of it home to drink.

Sometimes these 'oases' are discovered purely by chance. In 1881, Captain Neal Curry and his crew of 32 were forced to abandon their ship when it caught fire off the west coast of Mexico. The three lifeboats drifted for days in the hot sun. Debilitated by hunger and thirst, people began to lose consciousness. One night Curry dreamed that the sea around them had changed from blue to green and he was astonished to find it sweet to drink. On waking, he found that the water around the lifeboats was indeed green and, just as he had dreamed, it was fresh and drinkable. Enough to keep them alive until they landed on the Mexican coast.

Spring water of the highest quality was esteemed by tea connoisseurs of the T'ang Dynasty. The tea masters compiled a list of the twenty best 'waters from heaven', grading springs in order of excellence. Their texts assert that fine tea achieves its peak of perfection when brewed with spring water from the district where the tea is grown. This tradition continues at Hangchow where tea shops serve local Dragon's Well Tea made with water from the famous spring of the same name.

The Jade Spring of Peking, situated about 10 kilometres (6 miles) from the city, was the source most favoured by the Imperial family for their teas and soups. After thousands of years it remains as pristine as ever. Visiting it in 1991, John Blofield wrote in *The Chinese Art of Tea*: 'Peking's Jade Spring has the clearest water I have ever seen. The pool it feeds is exceedingly deep, yet the tiniest fronds of underwater vegetation covering the bottom are visible to people seated in the shadow of an ancient pagoda on its bank. It would be easy to believe that such water had magical qualities!'

New York sits above a network of mineral springs once highly prized by native Indians and settlers alike. James Reuel Smith so loved the springs of New York that he spent four years at the close of the nineteenth century riding around on his bicycle photographing and documenting every spring he could find. His encyclopaedic work, *Springs and Wells of Manhattan and the Bronx, New York City*, contains 154 photographs and extensive detail. The most famous watering place at the time was Tanner's Spring in Central Park West, where Dr Henry Tanner lived on its waters alone during a forty-day fast.

Such springs were treated with respect, unlike their modern manifestations. In 1957, the journal *Engineering News-Record* told of a huge gush of water that spurted from the ground when builders were digging the foundations of an extension to Harlem Hospital. It flowed continuously at a rate of 8000 litres (1760 gallons) per minute and throughout a bitterly cold winter its temperature held steady at 20°C (68°F). Officials from the Department of Water, Gas and Electricity were never able to trace its origin, despite pumping green dye into nearby sewers and reservoir outlets. Hospital chemists who analysed the water found it as pure as any mountain spring. Finally, the outlet was plugged with massive concrete blocks, and the building's shell had to be reinforced to cope with the water pressure. In a more enlightened age, the hospital might have incorporated the spring into its treatment facilities.

In the deserts of the Middle East, springs are rare and treasured. The sudden appearance of water in the dry sand is a miracle worth celebrating. The Water of Paradise, a Sufic parable from the ninth-century sage Abu el-Atahiyya, is the story of Harith, a poor Bedouin who lived in a remote Persian desert with his wife Nafisa and their solitary camel. It was a hard life; they trapped desert rats, eating their flesh, and selling the skins to passing traders. Shallow pools of brackish water supplied enough for their daily needs.

One day, Harith found a new spring seeping up from the sand near his camp. Scooping some up in his hand he sipped it slowly and carefully. After the water he was used to drinking this was so cool and refreshing that Harith imagined it must resemble that which streams from the Springs of Paradise. He filled two goatskins and set off on his camel for Baghdad, several days distant. Upon reaching the city the dusty traveller presented himself at the Palace of Haroun el-Rashid saying that he had a rare gift for the Caliph. It was a day of public audience so Harith waited patiently until his turn came.

'Commander of the Faithful,' Harith began, 'I am a travelling Bedouin who has tasted many waters in the desert lands, but this,' he said, proudly holding up his battered goatskin, 'this is surely the Water of Paradise. May I respectfully present this offering as a gift from your most humble servant.'

Haroun the Straightforward poured some into a crystal goblet and drank. It tasted unpleasantly salty with a musty odour, but the Caliph gave no sign of displeasure. Smiling, he instructed his servants to take Harith to another room until he could think of a suitable reward.

Then he called the captain of his guards and said, 'What is nothing to us, is everything to him. He has brought the most precious thing he has and given it with love. Therefore, take him by night from the palace so that he does not see the mighty river Tigris. Escort him all the way to his tent and do not let him taste any sweet water on the way. Then give him my thanks and a thousand gold pieces. Tell him that he is the guardian of the Water of Paradise, that he may dispense freely to travellers in my name.'

Respect and reverence for water and springs is deeply embedded in the traditions of Islam. Within the Grand Mosque of Mecca, not 20 metres (65 feet) from the famous Black Stone, is the Zamzam spring whose water is carried home by pilgrims to all corners of the world. It dates from the time Ismael and his Egyptian mother Hagar were abandoned by Abraham to die in the desert. Having drunk all the water in the goatskin the patriarch had left them, they were about to give up hope when God heard their prayers and a powerful spring gushed from the ground making the sound, 'Zam, zam'.

The spring is prolific, enough to supply thousands of pilgrims who queue patiently everyday. The flow has been diverted to underground galleries with faucets that can supply many people at once. Described as having a 'refreshing and agreeable' taste, the waters of Zamzam are regarded by many Muslims as a universal remedy for ills of the body and spirit. To drink its waters bestows divine grace, to dip ones shroud in it, a blessing.

Which brings to mind another holy spring of more recent vintage, the Grotto of Lourdes where Christians queue in equal numbers with equal reverence for water infused with miraculous qualities.

In February 1858 Bernadette Soubirous, gathering driftwood by the banks of the river heard the sound of wind and looking up, saw in a niche among the rocks the figure of a girl bathed in golden light. Bernadette called her 'Acquero', 'That One'. Acquero appeared to Bernadette 17 times. When asked for her name she replied, 'I am the Immaculate Conception', words now inscribed beneath her statue in the grotto. On one of Bernadette's visits, Acquero told her to 'go and drink at the spring and wash in it'. When Bernadette scraped the damp floor of the grotto, water seeped into the hole she had made. This spring now provides around 40,000 litres (9000 gallons) of good quality water daily.

The church and state authorities were sceptical about the visions of Bernadette but, within a month, people were reporting miraculous cures for blindness, paralysis and terminal illness. The grotto was boarded up; cordons of police and soldiers turned away pilgrims; the Paris press lampooned and ridiculed the whole thing. The water was analysed by chemists who found that it contained 'no active ingredient capable of giving it distinct medicinal properties'. Believers welcomed this finding. If the water had no medicinal value, then its cures could only be attributed to divine intervention.

In 1862, four years after the first sighting, a commission of enquiry instigated by the Catholic Church verified Bernadette's version of the events. The grotto was opened and steps and platforms built. In 1876, a great Basilica was constructed. The wealth flowing into the town was spent on convents, hotels, hostels, parks, statues and a vast and imposing esplanade. During its first hundred years the spring attracted more than five million visitors. The great pilgrimages to Lourdes were rivalled only by those of medieval times. But was it the Virgin they came to commune with or was it the water? Do we see in the continuing stream of humanity that congregates at Lourdes each year, a revival of the ancient worship of springs and their female guardians, the nymphs? Was Acquero one of them?

The Spring of Immortality is another enduring story; the Fountain (from the Latin 'fons' meaning 'source') of Youth, from which the Water of Life flows without ceasing, obsessed kings, poets, artists and explorers. Chinese emperors sent fleets of ships to the east in search of the Isles of the Blessed where the spring was believed to flow. They never returned. No-one knew whether they were lost, wrecked or sunk in storms; or were the sailors living it up by the fountain on the fabled isle and in no mood to return?

Alexander the Great conquered the known world in his search for the magic spring he believed lay hidden in the remote glaciers of the Himalayas. He had heard stories of the Cow's Mouth, the glacial ice cave that is the source of the Ganges, worshipped by millions of Hindus. But he didn't get there in time to test its capacity to render him immortal; he died at the tender age of 33.

The Persian mystic saint Khydir actually found the Water of Life, so they say, but his compassionate nature proved to be his undoing. Khydir allowed his thirsty horse to drink first and then, before his astonished gaze, the crystal spring disappeared.

When the Inca Empire gradually fell to European invaders, the nobility sought refuge in a remote mountain settlement built around a spring which, like Lourdes and Zamzam, was a focus for religious and healing rituals. That spring flows at Vilcacamba, the Sacred Valley, in what is now Ecuador, and peasant descendants of the Inca fill their buckets and terracotta jars there. They've been drinking it all their lives, and some of these lives have been remarkably long, Vilcacamba has attracted the attention of researchers studying human ageing. Its residents are among the healthiest old people in the world. In 1992, the village had a population of 814, of which 15 per cent were more than 80 years old, 12 people exceeded 100 years and Jose Maria-Roa was still tilling his maize fields at the ripe old age of 132. To put this in some sort of perspective, only one person in every 1.7 million American citizens lives to be 100 or more. In Vilca-camba, it is one in 68. Dr Morton Walker's detailed study of the diet and lifestyle of its residents attributed their extraordinary longevity to the 'synergistic work-ings of the minerals in their drinking water.'

Maybe there is a Fountain of Youth after all. The only difficulty is that you have to drink it for your entire lifetime or it won't work, and there's no accom-modation for strangers in Vilcacamba, no TV, no night life. Everyone goes to bed early and rises with the sun. The alternative is to find your own spring or make a pilgrimage to one that appeals to you. Bring flowers and leave something of yourself behind, something small and personal, a thread from your clothing or a hair from your head. The rising sun is the best time to approach a spring if you wish to hear its voice. Empty yourself of all preconceptions, of thought even, and just sit.

This is how we learn from nature. If you stay long enough by a spring, watching its flowing, bubbling cascading motion, listening to its singing murmur, you may find that your mind will enter into communion with the water, with the soul of the spring. Then drink. Absorb its energy and power. This is the immortal fluid that has sustained the earth for millions of years.

And for this brief moment it flows for you.

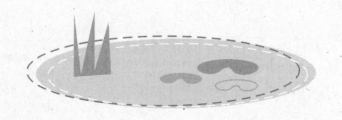

# The Enchanted Pond

The mirror of the pond reflects the shadows;
here is opened an entrance to the
mermaid's palace
. . . the moon shines through the willow trees
by the pond
where it washes its soul in the clear water.

Ji Cheng
*Yuan Ye*

Ponds are nature's mirrors in which we can see another world, another sun, other skies and our other selves. In puddles and ponds humans first saw themselves reflected. Having no knowledge of mirrors, they assumed that a spirit image was looking back at them out of the darkness of the water. This image made them fearful. If they looked at it for too long, the elders said, it could steal their soul.

Is it the stillness of the pond's reflective surface that enchants us and draws us into its dreaming?

Ancient Greeks believed that if you stared into a pond the spirits that lived there would drag your reflection down under the water leaving you soulless. Zulu people warn their children not to look into dark pools for the same reason. In Basutoland, crocodiles can steal your reflection, or even your shadow, causing you to die of unknown causes.

It was this sinister characteristic of ponds that led to the fall of Narcissus and his ill-fated admirer, Echo. Echo was an Oread, a nymph of mountains and grottos, who had been cursed to repeat the last words spoken to her. She fell in love with Narcissus, a handsome ego-centred Greek lad with many admirers, both male and female, but he treated them all with equal disdain, casting lovers aside as a tree sheds leaves in autumn. Echo followed Narcissus repeating his last words with as much affection as she could muster. Narcissus, embarrassed by this social liability, ignored her, turning away whenever she came near. Humiliated, Echo retreated to a cave where she wasted away until nothing was left but her voice, answering all who called.

One of Narcissus's other rejected suitors felt so sorry for Echo that he prayed to Nemesis asking that he who had been so indifferent to the love of others, should himself be tormented by a love from which he could expect no joy; he, too, should experience the grief of passion denied. As the divine guardian of moral and natural order, Nemesis took such requests seriously. It was his job to punish all who transgressed and, if possible, to make the punishment fit the crime.

One day Narcissus came upon a still clear pond in a forest glade. Thirsty from the fierce heat of the day, he lay on his stomach at the water's edge to drink. As he did so he saw his own face looking back at him. Narcissus had never seen anyone so beautiful. Overcome with desire, his heart went out to the handsome stranger. But whenever he stood up, the image disappeared. He couldn't bear to leave. The enchanted youth eventually became so disturbed that he lost his reason and died there by the pond, where Nemesis transformed his body into the sweet-scented white and golden flowers that bear his name.

The authors of the thirteenth-century allegory, *The Romance of the Rose*, use the story of Narcissus and the reflective pond to caution the reader against vanity and self-love. The pond is, they say, 'the perilous mirror in which proud Narcissus gazed . . . whoever admires himself in this mirror can have no protection, no physician, since anything he sees with his eyes puts him on the road to love. This mirror has put many a valiant man to death, for the wisest, most intelligent and carefully instructed are all surprised and captured here. Out of this mirror a new madness comes upon men.'

Some ponds can have quite the opposite effect. They may equally be agents of healing, contemplation and transformation. Leslie Silko's *Ceremony* tells the story of the rehabilitation of an emotionally damaged North American Indian Vietnam veteran. At one point he finds himself sitting beside a pond watching the frogs and insects, remembering the stories he had been told as a child.

> The spider came out first. She drank from the
> edge of the pool careful to keep the delicate
> egg sac on her abdomen out of the water . . .
> He remembered stories about her . . . She
> alone had known how to outsmart the mali-
> cious mountain Ka't'sina who imprisoned
> the rain clouds in the northwest room of his

> magical house . . . Dragonflies came and
> hovered over the pool. They were all colours
> of blue—powdery sky blue, dark night blue,
> shimmering with almost black iridescent
> light, and mountain blue. There were stories
> about dragonflies too. He turned. Everywhere
> he looked he saw a world made of stories, the
> long ago, time immemorial stories.

Dragonflies have always fascinated me. Their intense colours, particularly the red ones, their speed and manoeuvrability, the way they seem to patrol their territory. I could watch them for hours and sometimes do.

Zuni Indians credit the dragonfly with supernatural powers and healing abilities. Their ceremonial wooden dragonfly masks have small eyes, which pregnant women are warned not to look at lest they bear a child with eye problems. The Somaikoli (Dragonfly) Society of the Zuni is renowned for curing disorders of the eye. The head of a dragonfly consists mostly of two massive eyes, each with 28,000 lenses (compared to 4000 in the eye of a housefly). These eyes have watched the creation of the world as we know it. When a dark blue dragonfly landed on the tip of my index finger while I was sitting near its pool, it was a deliberate act of interest. Slowly I lifted my hand and looked into those amazing eyes. Two hundred and fifty million years of evolution on my fingertip stared back at me. It stayed for a minute or two, every second precious, before continuing on its way.

Another pond dweller laden with ancient significance is the frog.

In order to get to know frogs more intimately I built a small pond outside my bedroom window. A friend warned me against this. She said the frog chorus would keep me awake at night. But I liked the idea of being serenaded by frogs. I wanted their company, their energy, their tireless enthusiasm.

Now the pond is home to purple irises, white lilies and a single lotus. And a frog with a most peculiar song which would have enchanted the American composer John Cage. 'Dock', it calls every six seconds, with the regularity of a dripping tap, 'dock'. My frog books tell me this is the serenade of the Striped Marsh Frog (*Lymnodynastes peroni*). They describe the sound as that of a hammer tapping a loose plank—'dock'. One night the calls increased in tempo and volume— 'dock, dock, dock, dock'. Then I realised there must be two of them. Their mating kept them (and me) awake for hours. In the morning the fruit of their labours, hundreds of frogs' eggs floated in white froth among the lilies.

Frogs and ponds are inseparable, their connection celebrated by the witty nature-loving poet monks of

Japanese Zen. In the eighteenth century, Kobayashi Issa wrote:

> A moonlit evening: here beside the pool,
> Stripped to the waist, a frog enjoys the cool.

Another enduring pond/frog haiku is that of the seventeenth-century master, Bashô.

> The old green pond is silent; here the hop
> Of a frog plumbs the evening stillness: plop!

Frogs have been doing this for millions of years—hopping in and out of ponds. Their ability to change from one life form to another, from egg to tadpole to four-legged land dweller, has elevated frogs to the status of deities.

The swamp was the symbolic image of Egyptian precosmic reality from which eight primordial gods, the Ogdoad, created the world. After they retired to the Underworld, the Ogdoad caused the Nile to flow and the sun to rise. The four male deities are shown with the heads of frogs, the four females, serpents, all dwelling in the fecund pond of creation.

The water goddess Heket is represented as a frog. The divine midwife at the birth of the world, Heket was the guardian of pregnant women who wore her image as a protective amulet. In a temple at Abydos, the Pharoah makes offerings to Heket in her frog incarnation, invoking her power to give life to the dead. Embalmed frogs were laid beside with human mummies in Egyptian tombs to accompany them in their journey to the other world.

'Frogs do for the night what birds do for the day: they give it a voice. And the voice is a varied and stirring one,' wrote the Florida naturalist, Archie Carr in his *Celebration of Eden* (1994). The song of the frogs is a hymn to the waters. The name of the Mayan rain god Chac is a frog call. Frogs sang the first songs made by vocal cords. One music critic described them as 'the richest sonic symphonies in today's ecosystem!'

Living in a bungalow among the rice paddies of Bali, I was initially mystified by the cacophony of sound coming from the water at night. Not just croaking, but groans and grunts and nightbird calls. It was the frogs, my landlord told me. The range and variety were astonishing. Some frogs sing in choruses of 1000 that can be heard miles away. During the American colonists war with the French, residents of a small Connecticut village are said to have evacuated when they mistook the distant cries of frogs for the oncoming enemy.

During the Middle Ages, servants were sent to throw stones into nearby ponds at night to silence the frogs so that the lord of the manor could get to sleep. Even today in Britain, the chorus of frogs around the town pond has sometimes 'roused whole villages to indignation'. Describing such a pond in *Cannery Row*, John Steinbeck wrote: 'There were frogs there all right, thousands of them. Their voices beat the night, they boomed and barked and croaked and rattled. They sang to the stars, to the waning moon, to the waving grasses. They bellowed love songs and challenges.'

Some ponds are home to powerful wind and rain deities. At the base of the great red rock of Uluru in Central Australia lies the spring-fed pool of Mutitjilda, home of the Rainbow Serpent. It is dangerous to disturb him. Another pond-dwelling serpent is the spiral spirit of the tornado, the water goddess the Zulu people of South Africa call the Inkanyamba. Manifesting herself as a giant spinning snake of enormous size, the Inkanyamba rises out of her pool and stretches up to the heavens, bringing rain, hail and storms, destroying everything in her path.

Once a man was picked up by the Inkanyamba and carried back to her pool. No-one could find him. Then a shaman who had knowledge of these things offered his help. He went to the pool when the Inkanyamba was away, dived in and persuaded the man who had adapted to life underwater to return to land. When both men emerged from the water, it was seen that this 'water person' had long hair like seagrass and a flowing white beard. He was strong and healthy but refused cooked food, eating only crabs, fish and frogs.

The Inkanyamba returned and, finding her man missing, went to look for him. This caused such terrible storms that the chiefs asked the man to give himself up as a sacrifice. He did so cheerfully, they say, since he no longer enjoyed life on earth. As soon as he returned the storms subsided.

Then there's the bunyip.

When the first Europeans came to Australia they saw strange creatures they'd never seen before: the duck-billed platypus, koalas, kangaroos, goannas and giant Murray cod. So they weren't surprised when indigenous people told of a giant man-eating creature that lived in ponds, swamps and billabongs. *The Sydney Gazette* of 1812 called this monster a *Bahnyip*: 'a large black animal like a seal, with a terrible voice which creates terror among the blacks'. It was known by many names in Aboriginal languages, but the most popular appellation was *bunyip*.

Bunyips are solitary monsters of variable size that inhabit 'gruesome pools locked in the grotesque arms of hoary gums and shadowed by she-oaks'. Many claimed to have seen the creatures. Many more were transfixed by their dreadful booming roar echoing in the bush on moonless nights.

Sceptics who doubted the existence of bunyips pointed to the seals and sea-lions which had occasionally been found a thousand kilometres or more inland. The sound, they said, was made by a water bird, the Brown Bittern (*Botaurus poiciloptlus*) whose cry was similar to that attributed to the bunyip. But Australians had fallen in love with bunyips and they became part of the folklore of the bush. Outback children, both black and white, were entertained and terrified by bunyip stories, which adults found useful for calming the unruly and the reckless. 'The bunyip will get you' was a potent reminder to youngsters not to stray too far from campfire or homestead.

In North America and Africa, ponds were often venues for ceremonies connected with water. In his autobiography, *Of Water and the Spirit*, African shaman Malidoma Patrice Somé describes his initiation at a crystal-clear pool deep inside a mountain cave. 'This water has been here since time immemorial,' says the leading elder. 'It protects the doorway to the ancestors . . . This water is the roof of a world you are going to visit for a while . . . There is no bottom as there is in the village river, instead there is a world . . .'

Somé tells how he plunged into the pool and passed through into this 'other' world where he became 'a shapeless consciousness in the middle of a misty presence that was everywhere around me'. A benign presence made itself felt, one which poured 'information into my heart'. After several hours, Somé found himself back in the cave standing in the pool, his face wet with tears, his mind filled with the essence of the Spirit.

At the heart of the south Indian city of Madurai lies the Pond of the Golden Lotus. Surrounded by the vast Meenakshi Temple complex, this pond was worshipped long before the massive monuments and columns were built. Indeed, it is the reason for their existence. Situated on the banks of the sacred Vaigai River, Madurai is one of the sub-continent's oldest cities. By the third century BC the fame of Madurai and its pond had spread to Greece and Rome and it attracted cosmopolitan pilgrims and visitors. We know this because Megasthenes, the Greek ambassador to India at that time, left us many lively anecdotes and descriptions of Indian religious practices in his *Ta Indika* (310 BC).

I had come to learn more about this marvellous pool, which was associated with the Golden Age of Tamil literature at a time when my Norse and Scot ancestors were still running around in animal skins.

The Pond of the Golden Lotus attracted so many people that it became necessary to enclose it within a walled perimeter with marble steps leading down to the water. The entire structure is known as a 'tank'.

Since this particular tank is an acre in area the result is rather like a large amphitheatre with the pond at its centre.

On these stone steps the Tamil *Sangham*, an academy of writers, scholars and poets, met regularly. When one felt that he had written a poem or story worthy of being submitted for judgement, he rose and read the composition to his assembled peers. Then the aspirant walked to the water's edge and placed his handwritten palm-leaf text on the surface of the pond. Everyone watched and waited. If the manuscript floated, it was judged to be a work of merit; otherwise it sank to the bottom along with the author's self-esteem.

Such was the wisdom of the water that this practice continued for centuries, during which time the pond selected some of the finest works in the Tamil language, books and poems still read at ceremonies performed around the Golden Lotus tank. How many airport novels or learned academic theses would survive this sort of scrutiny, I thought, looking down at the still water.

I had come with a partner to Madurai and while she tirelessly visited other temples and holy places, I found myself returning day after day to the Meenakshi Temple gate where a long queue waited to present their offerings of fruit to the temple elephant. The elephant takes each gift in his trunk, carefully puts it in a cane basket beside his seated human attendant then slowly swings his trunk back to kiss you ever so sweetly on the forehead.

It's hard to explain just how blissful that feels. I burst into tears the first time the elephant kissed me. And next day, there I was back in the queue clutching a small bunch of bananas, waiting patiently for my morning kiss before passing through to the tank beyond.

The tank is awash with pilgrims, 25,000 on a busy day. Some come to bathe, others collect its holy essence in jars and bottles. Many more sit after their long journey, content to absorb the water's energy and bathe in the aura of devotion.

I was one of these.

Beside me on the cool marble floor of the shaded collonade sat Sanpat, an old grey-bearded man in spotlessly clean white robes. When I first arrived looking for somewhere to sit, Sanpat gestured to a spot on his mat and I accepted. He told me many stories. Often we sat together in silence looking out over the water.

The pond of Krishna and Radha is a sacred site a couple of hour's drive south of New Delhi. The Radhakund, the pond of Radha, in the land of Braj has been loved and revered for centuries. Its waters have absorbed an unimaginable flood of devotional energy. If any water could be said to be infused with spirit it is surely that of the Radhakund.

In the time when gods dwelt among humans, Krishna grew up in a rural village in Braj. As a teenager he played love games with the *Gopis*, the girls who looked after the cows. Radha appealed to Krishna more than the others. They soon became lovers.

When the wicked demon Arisha transformed himself into a raging black bull intent on wreaking havoc on the peaceful village of the cowherds, Krishna blocked his path. Without any hesitation the angry god ripped off the bull's horns and beat him to death with them. Later that evening Krishna wanders into the moonlit forest to meet Radha. When they come together, Radha smiles and modestly lowers her eyelashes. Planting a lace-painted hand on the blue god's chest, she firmly holds him at bay.

'Don't touch me,' she says in a teasing tone. 'Your hands have killed a bull. You are untouchable. Your breath smells of blood and battle. I will not make love with you until you cleanse yourself.'

Krishna is taken aback, but Radha is adamant.

'What must I do to make myself acceptable?' asks Krishna humbly.

'You must bathe in all the holy waters of all the sacred places,' Radha replies. 'Only this and nothing more . . . or less,' she adds.

What was an impatient god to do? Krishna has a sudden lightning flash of inspiration. Lifting his left foot he stamps his heel into the ground, making a deep hole. Then, using his divine power, he summons the holy waters from all the sacred places to come together to fill the imprint. When the pond filled, Krishna immersed himself, washed away the taint of pollution and emerged cleansed and refreshed. Smiling, Radha drew him down on the soft moss among the shadows . . .

But, being the boastful character that he is, Krishna has to ruin his romantic triumph by boasting about how he'd made this marvellous pond, just by stamping his foot. An angry Radha summons the girl cowherds to her mud hut. 'Women's business,' she tells them. 'We will make our own pond, even if we have to dig it out with our bare hands!' And they do. However, the hole they dig so industriously remains dry. No water fills it. Radha's resolve is undiminished. 'We will fill it ourselves,' she tells her supporters. They set up a bucket brigade between their hole and the nearest holy water, a pond called Manasi Ganga. Manasi Ganga was an earlier creation of Krishna's, filled with the water of Mother Ganges. Every day the singing gopis fill their earthenware pots at the Manasi Ganga, pass them to one another, and empty them into Radha's pond. But no matter how hard they work the water soaks into the parched earth and drains away.

Not wanting to see his beloved humiliated, Krishna secretly fills her receptacle with the water of his heart. And thus the Radhakund came into being.

'The sweetness of the pond is the sweetness of Radha. The greatness of the pond is her greatness. They are one and the same,' asserted the saint Chaitanya after he had bathed in the water. Indeed it was Chaitanya who rediscovered the location of the long lost pond after being led to the spot in a vision. The Radhakund was excavated and cleaned in 1546 and Krishna's pond, the Shyamkund, seven years later.

Devotees bathe and drink, float flowers on the ponds, chant the story songs of the divine couple as they write the holy names on their bodies using mud from the bank. To those who worship them, the ponds are manifestations of divinity, simultaneous aquatic representations of duality and unity. Radha and Krishna are depicted in popular devotional posters standing, their limbs intertwined. The rationale for this is symbolic. Since love cannot take place in formless unity, in order for a god to experience the pains and joys of the senses, an earthly body is needed. Sensual love needs two. It is for this, say the Hindu scriptures, that non-dual reality splits and becomes two—in order to experience love as mortals do.

'In the beginning,' *The Upanishads* tell us, 'Krishna the supreme reality was filled with the desire to create. By his own will he assumed a twofold form. From the left half arose a woman, the right half became a man. The male figure was Krishna himself; the female was the Primordial Nature Goddess, Radha.'

The ponds are separated by a causeway linked by a subterranean passage which allows their waters to mingle. Thus Radhakund and Shyamkund share one liquid, the nectar of Krishna.

But the water of love is not to be found in any one specific geographical location. Since all water is connected, all water is the water of love, of compassion, of immortality.

All we need to do is drink.

# Take Me to the River

Thou river who didst create all things,
When the great gods dug thee out
They set prosperity upon thy banks.
Within thee the King of the Deep
has made his dwelling.
Thou judgest the cause of mankind.
O River, thou art mighty. O River, thou art supreme.
O River, thou art righteous.

Ancient Babylonian prayer to the Euphrates

Lightning flashes from the brows of the terracotta statue of Great Mother Ishtar as she stands in a glass case in the museum at Aleppo in Syria. Wrapped around her waist is a river in which fish swim up towards the everflowing waterpot she holds out to the world.

The waterpot is a recurring symbol of the source of rivers, the point of origin, the fountainhead. The *Kumbh Mela*, the Festival of the Waterpot, is held in India every 12 years to honour the divinity of rivers. In 2001, thirty million people came to bathe and pray. It was the largest gathering in human history. The *Mela* celebrates the battle between gods and demons over the water pot (*kumbh*) that holds the water of immortality churned up from the bed of the ocean. Ultimately, of course, the gods win but during the struggle four drops of the precious fluid fell on the places where the *Mela* is celebrated.

Religions are divided about river symbolism. Some see the source as a holy place while others focus on the flow of rivers towards the great ocean of awareness. Personally I am attracted to the source.

High in the mountains of Bali is Tirta Empul, the spring where the Parisan river begins. The temple complex that surrounds it, built by a Hindu king a thousand years ago, has been continually reconstructed, the spring itself enclosed by a moss-covered stone wall. I stood for hours looking at the water welling powerfully up out of the dark sand. Its continuous flow offered such a graphic vision of infinite mystery that all other thought dissolved. Being present at the birth of a river is a rare and precious experience.

For as long as anyone can remember, rivers have been worshipped as living entities, sacred, holy and beneficent. Early humans found that rivers formed natural boundaries, part of a divine scheme for limiting conflict by creating and defining borders. The word 'river' is derived from the verb 'to rive' which means to 'divide' or 'split asunder'. Historically, rivers have often served as borders between nations, states, and tribal areas, geographically delineating frontiers, defining territories and, by doing so, preventing disputes.

To bridge the natural boundary of the river was a defiant and sacrilegious act. The bridge builder risked offending the powerful river god by providing safe passage for those who might otherwise have drowned. For this reason, the Romans built only three bridges across the Tiber. To propitiate the river, the Romans conducted elaborate ceremonies and processions of dignitaries. Led by the Vestal Virgins, they culminated in casting 24 straw puppets of men, bound hand and foot, into the river. This was a vestige of an earlier and more brutal epoch when men aged over sixty, being unfit for military service, were tossed into the river and drowned.

The idea that rivers and bridges demand human sacrifices seems to have co-evolved with the rise of imperial power in Europe and China. There's no doubt that accidental drowning was seen by many as the river gods claiming their victims, but the idea of throwing people into the river to appease its spirit seems to be connected with the rise of kingdoms and empires. Fortunately, this custom disappeared over time.

But there are always diehards who cling obstinately to the old ways. In 1890, the *Pall Mall Gazette* warned its London readers thinking of visiting China that the heads of unwary travellers were being cut off and sold to the Department of Public Works for ten pounds each 'in order that they might be built into the foundations of the piers of a number of new bridges that are in the course of erection. Such is the terror of the coolies that for no money could they be induced to carry fares to the suburbs at night!'

In the early days of Rome the ritual drowning of criminals and miscreants in the Tiber was a common form of punishment. The Egyptians, on the other hand, saw drowning as a divine blessing, and the priests of the Nile buried with high honours all who drowned in the river. Since the god had claimed them, they were now his property.

For those who truly believe that the river is a divinity in liquid form, drowning is the most auspicious of deaths. Bishop Heber, visiting Benares in 1825, saw pilgrims going into the water, 'each having tied under his arms a pair of large pots with their wide mouths open. The vessels served as temporary floats, to carry the pilgrim into the centre of the stream; once safely launched, the man would splash the sacred water into the jars until they were full enough to sink, and pull him gently into eternity, his soul forever pure of earthly stain'.

Crossing a river before the time of bridges was a dangerous enterprise, an occasion for prayer and reflection. First one purified oneself, then communed with the spirit of the river and asked for permission to cross. The Greek poet Hesiod wrote a warning in his *Theogeny*: whoever attempted to cross without first cleansing his hands of the evil with which they were sullied, would attract the anger of the gods who would send down the direst punishment.

When the Greek army arrived at a river, sacrifices were offered to ascertain whether the omens were auspicious or not. In *The Persian Expedition*, Xenophon describes the famous crossing of the Centrites. 'On reaching the bank of the river where the ford was, they grounded arms, and then Chirisophus himself first put a ceremonial wreath on his head, threw aside his cloak and took up his arms, telling the rest to follow his example. He ordered the captains to lead their companies across in columns, some on the left and others on the right of him. The soothsayers then cut the throats of the animals over the river. This was so that the priests could note how the water received the blood and thus make the appropriate deductions about its mood.' Xenophon continues: 'The appearance of the victims was pronounced favourable, and then all the soldiers sang the paean and raised the battle-cry, and Chirisophus and his men went into the river.'

The Vala were Norse prophetesses who could read the destiny of men in flowing rivers. Plutarch explains that the Vala obtained their insights by listening to the sounds of streams and studying the eddies and currents of the waters. They travelled with armies whose leaders turned to them for advice. The predictions of the Vala were seldom questioned.

The Roman general Drusus was awed by the appearance of Velada, the white-robed woman who stood at the head of the wild Teutonic horde waiting for him on the other side of the Elbe. 'Calamity will befall you if you attempt to cross this river,' she screamed at him brandishing a long ornamental dagger. The powerful Roman army, before whom Europe trembled, turned around and went home.

But there are always those who think they are above the law.

When Cyrus, the Persian, set out to attack the city of Babylon in 539 BC, he came to the river Gyndus. While the emperor was making preparations for a crossing, Amodais, one of his favourite white Arab stallions, lost his footing on the bank and was swept away in the powerful current. The river god had taken another victim. Cyrus was angry. This was a challenge to the Imperial prestige. He decided to punish the river, to show the world who was really in charge here.

Cyrus put his entire army to work building a giant hydraulic masterpiece, a barrier that divided the mighty Gyndus into 360 separate channels, each shallow enough to be crossed 'by a woman without wetting her knees'. It made no difference to the river, however. Shallow or deep it continued on its way.

Rivers are living symbols of universal potentiality, of the fluidity of forms, of purification, fertility, death and renewal. Rivers have much to teach us about life, living and selflessness.

'The highest benevolence is like that of water' observed the philosopher Lao Zi standing on the banks of the Yellow River; 'The benevolence of water is to benefit all beings without strife.'

Under the signs of K'an, the Great Abyss, the 3000-year-old Chinese oracle, *The Book of Changes*, offers the image of moving water as an example of appropriate action in a time of crisis.

> Man finds himself in danger, like water in the depths of an abyss. The water shows him how to behave: it flows on without piling up anywhere, and even in dangerous places it does not lose its dependable character. In this way, danger is overcome . . .

> Water is constant in its flow . . . and just as water flows on and on, the wise man makes use of its practice in his teaching.

All water is alive, but by virtue of its very movement it is infused with additional power and strength. Life is motion, vibration and change, just as the water of a river is constantly changing from second to second. When we meditate on rivers, our consciousness merges with that of the waters; freed from the artificial self-imposed constraints of time and space, we encounter that which cannot be measured. The Zen patriarch Hui Neng taught his disciples that the far bank across the ever-flowing river was *pāramitā*, awaiting our awareness of its presence.

Some travellers are more aware than others that crossing to the far bank may bring unforeseen difficulties. Early one dark morning, a group of devout

Hindus set out in a long boat to cross the Ganges. Their destination was a Shiva Temple where the rituals began at dawn. Tired, cold and hungry, the pilgrims kept their spirits up by smoking a little hashish, a practice not uncommon among devotees in India. They rowed hard against the strong current for what seemed like hours, but still the farther shore seemed as distant as ever. Then the first light revealed their mistake. In their stoned confusion, they had forgotten to untie the long rope that tethered the boat to the wharf.

I was told this story many years ago by an Indian Vipassana teacher. The point of the parable was that no matter how much effort and energy we expend in the spiritual or material world, unless we free ourselves from the constraints of false perception and old attachments, we will never reach our destination.

Another river of mythic significance in terms of memorable crossings is the Rubicon.

The Rubicon is not exactly a river. It's a small stream that flows through the Apennine Mountains near the miniature state of San Marino. In 49 BC it formed the political border between Roman-occupied Gaul and the rest of Italy. Gaul at the time was governed by its conquerer, Caius Julius Caesar. Back in Rome, his partners Pompey and Crassus, feeling threatened, intrigued against him. When

Crassus died in 58 BC, Pompey became sole consul and immediately requested that the Senate demand Caesar's resignation from his army command.

Caesar did not comply. Instead, as a public show of treason and defiance, he crossed the Rubicon and marched on Rome. Pompey fled. And the rest is history. The phrase 'Crossing the Rubicon' has come to mean taking decisive action that commits one to a dangerous enterprise.

The mythic River of Life, which originates at a mysterious source in the misty mountains and winds its way through the valleys and plains until it merges with the ocean, is an ever-present reminder of the eternal flow of *chi* or *prana*, of the transience of human existence and its inevitable passage from birth to death.

'All rivers are sacred,' the holy books of India remind us, 'all flow towards the sea; all are like mothers to the world, all purge away sins.' Female divinity was associated with rivers at an early stage of human development. A 7000-year-old terracotta urn found near Belgrade in Yugoslavia portrays the goddess as a water container decorated with running spirals and meandering lines in the form of 'Ms' or 'Ws'. On the neck of the jar, her impassive face appears above a large 'M' symbol.

The first pictograms represented water as a flowing entity, as a spiral (manifested in seashells and ammonites) or as a continuous M-shaped line. The Egyptians adopted this as the hieroglyph for *Mer*, meaning both 'water' and 'mother love'. The Hebrews designated water as *Mem*, while ancient Arab languages used the word *Ma* for water, for mother and for the name approximating Mary. The Celtic *Mare* links the symbolic images of water, horse and female.

In *A Mystical Key to the English Language*, Robert Hoffstein suggests that the word '*memory*' originates from '*Mem*' (the waters) linked with the sun in its symbolic form '*or*' (gold, golden) and/or '*aurum*' (halo). 'Therefore,' he says 'our memories can be seen as "watery slates" reflecting the images of life, poetically rendered as the "or" or golden sun.'

The great rivers of India are all addressed as *Mai*, mother. 'I come to you as a child to his mother,' begins a famous pilgrims' prayer to the Ganges:

I come as an orphan to you, moist with love.
I come without refuge to you, giver of sacred
rest.
I come a fallen man to you, uplifter of all.
I come undone by disease to you, the perfect
physician.
I come, my heart dry with thirst, to you,
ocean of sweet wine.
Do with me whatever you will.

The Russian river Volga is *Mat' Rodnaya*, 'Mother of the Land', while the Thai words '*mae nan*' translate literally as 'mother water'. The annual floods of the Nile are the tears of Mother Isis. The Irish rivers Boyne and Shannon contain the names of the Celtic goddesses Boinn and Sinainn, the Scottish Clyde comes from Clõta, the 'Divine Washer' and the Welsh river Dee honours Dêvã, 'the holy goddess'. The influences of the Celtic religions can be seen in the French river Marne whose name derives from *Matrona*, 'Divine Mother', from which the designation of Matron also arises. The Matronae were deities of ancient Gaul.

At the source of the Seine in a valley near Châtillon in Burgundy, the Sequanae, a Celtic tribe, erected a temple and healing sanctuary to honour their spiritual mother, Sequana, goddess of the river. A bronze image of Sequana discovered nearby shows her standing in a boat with the head and tail of a duck. Pilgrims bathed in a spring-fed pool at the main temple and cast carved wooden images of themselves, or the personification of their ailment, into the water as offerings and tokens of gratitude. So far, two hundred votive offerings have been recovered from the site and displayed along with other Celtic treasures at the Musée Archeologique in Dijon.

The elders of the Ijo in Nigeria keep alive their creation story of Mother Woyengi who came down to earth in a flash of lightning and immediately set to work making people out of clay. As she breathed life into each one, she offered them the opportunity to choose their gender and their future lifestyle.

When she had completed her task, Mother Woyengi led her animated creations to a place where two rivers flowed side by side. She spoke in a voice of thunder. 'The river on the right,' she said gesturing with her hand, 'leads to luxury, riches, fame and fortune; the river on the left leads to humble, helpful creative work. Go where you will.' Those who entered the river of luxury found it deep and fast-flowing, with dangerous currents and subterranean weeds that clutched at their legs. The river of humility, on the other hand, was shallow, clean and clear. And so it was that the children of Woyengi entered the stream of luxury or that of humility, and were carried away to irrigate the human race.

Another creation story from Nigeria tells how Princess Oya manifested the river we foreigners call the Niger.

When an invading army threatened the Nupe people, the King called on the services of an oracle known as the Ifa. 'Could the enemy be stopped?' he asked the visionary. 'How can the kingdom be saved?'

The oracle instructed the King to send for a length of black cloth and then find a virgin to tear it in half.

The cloth was quickly procured, but finding a suitable female whose virginity was a hundred per cent verifiable was more difficult. Time was running out. The King decided that this own daughter would perform the ceremony. The young woman took the black cloth in both hands and *O-ya*, 'she tore' it apart and threw the two pieces on the ground in front of the assembled tribe, whereupon the cloth turned into two streams of black water which flowed around the kingdom, now an island in the midst of Oya's river.

Oya's island is a holy place. The story of how it came to be is passed down from generation to generation. Even now the Cuban descendants of Yoruba slaves still talk of Oya's Island as a place of return for the souls of the dead, where they will be at peace, a place from which their spirits may be recalled to bless the living.

While every river in China had its own spirit, one was pre-eminent in myth, legend and literature—He Bo, Lord of the Yellow River, to whom even the Emperor bowed his head. He Bo was a mortal who had dedicated himself to the river by jumping in loaded down with stones, thus achieving immortality.

Rulers called on He Bo to witness their oaths and presented him with girls of royal blood as bride sacrifices. The cult of He Bo continued for centuries but gradually its character changed. Instead of princesses who, after all, had better things to do, a girl of low birth but great beauty was chosen. Her parents were powerless to protest. The choosing of the bride was the responsibility of a college of sorcerers and magicians dedicated to raising money and generally managing the affairs of the river god in the city of Ye. The proclamation was made a year in advance so that everyone had time to prepare. On the 'marriage' day, the girl, dressed in elaborate bridal robes, was taken by palanquin to the temple on the river bank where the feast and celebrations took place. At its conclusion she was placed on a marriage bed of embroidered silk packed tightly with straw and launched into the current where she slowly sank.

In the fourth century, Simen Bao, a newly-appointed magistrate, asked if he could attend the marriage ceremony in his official capacity. The shamans were delighted and prepared a place of honour for him. As the festivities got under way, Bao had the presiding priestess of the cult brought before him.

'I have seen the face of this girl,' he said, 'and she is not beautiful enough to marry a god. We must find another more suitable.'

'But the Lord of the River awaits his bride, everything is prepared. The time is auspicious,' re-joined the shamana. 'We cannot delay.'

'Then go to him yourself and explain why. I'm sure he will understand,' and with that Bao had his servants throw the priestess off the embankment into the river where she quickly sank. The crowd watched in astonishment.

'We will await her return,' said Bao calmly. 'Let the feast continue.'

An hour passed then Bao stood up 'Why does she stay so long? 'Something must have happened,' he announced. 'We must discover why the priestess has not come back to us.'

Turning to the marriage celebrants, he chose two more priestesses. 'Go and find out why your mistress has not returned,' and they too were cast into the river.

Then Bao reflected aloud that perhaps these women lacked the expertise and sophistication to intercede with the god, so he had the principal bureaucrat of the cult, a male, thrown in to help straighten out any misunderstanding.

At that point, the rest of the wedding 'organisers' fell to their knees, banged their heads on the ground until the blood flowed, confessed their transgressions and begged for mercy. 'The river god detains his guests too long,' said Bao. 'It is time for us to depart,' and with that he and his retinue returned home.

The ceremony was never performed again.

★

Stretching for 6900 kilometres (4300 miles) the Mississippi is one of the longest rivers in the world. It drains an area greater than the whole of Europe, if you exclude Russia, Norway and Sweden, and carries an annual load of 400 million tonnes of mud and silt into the Gulf of Mexico. Like all rivers, the Mississippi is constantly on the move, sideways, sometimes for miles, constantly reasserting the meandering loops that characterise the unobstructed passage of flowing water, travelling twice as far as it would if it flowed in a straight line.

Water writes these snake-like patterns on plains and mountains alike, patiently carving its curves into stone and sand. Any aerial photograph of a 'free' river, one whose banks have not been modified by human intervention, will illustrate the point. But why does water do this? Deliberately, persistently, it traces its signature over and over, its path of preference.

Could it be a conscious decision? Can water really assert itself? Of course it can and it has good sound reasons for so doing. Since water purifies itself by movement, then it follows that an increase in its length will reduce its load of contaminants. Or maybe it just likes to take the long way round—just for fun.

You can see this whenever a stream makes its way across a sandy beach to the ocean beyond. Initially, after rain, when the flow from A to B is at high volume, the stream pattern may be relatively straight but gradually, hour by hour, curves and loops assert themselves as water demonstrates that it has a mind of its own.

The word *meander* meaning 'a winding stream' comes from the Greek, *Maender*, a river that rises in Turkish Anatolia and flows west into the Aegean Sea. Its serpentine twists and turns are, mythically, the manifestation of the guilt of a distraught Greek general.

General Maeander found himself in a difficult position. His invasion of Phrygia in central Asia had stalled and it seemed as if defeat was imminent. In the inner sanctum of the Temple of Cybele, Maeander offered the goddess a deal. In the unlikely event of his winning the war with the Phrygians, he would give to the bloodthirsty deity as sacrifices the first three people to congratulate him on his return to Athens.

And who were first to welcome the conquering hero home? His mother, father and younger sister. Not one to renege on a sacred vow, Maeander sacrificed his family, then hurled himself into the river where his restless spirit writhes in perpetual remorse.

Another memorable Greek river is the Selemnos, whose waters have the power to extinguish the flames of unrequited love.

Selemnos was a handsome young shepherd who made the fatal mistake of drinking from a spring inhabited by Argyra, a passionate Naiad. Attracted by his rugged good looks, Argyra emerged from the water wearing little more than a winsome grin and invited the excited lad to sport with her on the soft green moss while his flocks grazed peacefully nearby.

Selemnos didn't realise the danger he was in.

Naiads are the daughters of Zeus and Thetis who live in fountains, springs and streams. Midday is their 'witching hour' when they appear in human form to enchant unwary mortals. It is said that Naiads can steal your soul, that those who see them become possessed thereafter by an uncontrollable 'nympholeptic mania', an obsessive fascination that troubles the spirit and destroys the character.

Incidentally, this is the origin of the term 'nympho-mania' used by sex-obsessed psychiatrists in the nineteenth century to medicalise women overcome with such an excess of desire that it could not easily be satisfied. The only cure for this clinical condition involved long and expensive sessions with male therapists.

Day after day Selemnos returned to make love with Argyra in the enchanted grove until, predictably, the restless Naiad lost interest. No longer entertained by the boy, she dived back into the spring and did not return.

Selemnos was devastated. He neglected his sheep, lost his job and spent his time moping miserably around the forest deeply depressed. So great was his distress that the love goddess Aphrodite, tired of his incessant weeping, transformed Selemnos into a crystal clear river and erased the image of Argyra forever from his memory. Thus it came to be said that bathing in the Selemnos or drinking its water slakes the passion of desire and frees one from the sorrow of lost love.

Now that's a water worth bottling if ever there was one.

We are constantly being told that our obsession with expensive bottles of water from 'pristine' mountain springs is a recent phenomenon. This is not true. The bottled water trade has a long history, but in the ancient world it was the water of certain rivers, not springs, that was in demand.

Worshipped as a god by the Egyptians and the Romans, the Nile was prized for its unique properties. Unlike the water of ordinary rivers, that of the Nile did not deteriorate with age. Aristides was amazed. 'The Egyptians,' he wrote 'alone of all the people we know fill jars with water as others do with wine and keep it at home for three or four or even more years, and point with pride to the date as we do with wine.' The memoirs of the Roman, Achilles Tatius, record his enthusiasm.

That was the first occasion on which I drank the water of the Nile without mixing it with wine, as I wished to test its excellence as a drink. Wine spoils its character. I filled a transparent glass with it and saw that in the matter of limpidity it vied with nay, it defeated the vessel that contained it. To the taste it is sweet and cool enough as to be delightful.

Nile water became so popular that soon there was a shortage of suitable containers.

Another award-winning bottled water in early times was drawn from the Ganges, whose water is the divine essence of the goddess, Ganga, come down to Earth in liquid form. Some say she flowed from the toe of Vishnu after a miraculous concert arranged by Narada. Narada was the messenger of the gods and a comic figure in Hindu scripture. He was also a part-time busker who is credited with the invention of the veena, a stringed instrument on which he accompanied himself. But no matter how hard he tried, Narada could never surpass the celestial music of the gods.

One day as Narada was strolling about playing and singing, he encountered a crowd of people heading in the opposite direction. What attracted his attention was that each one was missing an eye or an ear or a limb. 'What happened?' asked Narada, appalled. 'Who did this to you?' Their leader explained that they were divine spirits of music who had been maimed by Narada's appalling singing. 'Is there nothing I can do to restore your lost organs?' Narada responded anxiously. 'Can I repair the damage?'

'Only the song of the great Shiva can make us whole again,' the leader replied. Narada called on Shiva to ask him if he'd do it.

'Not right now,' said Shiva who was busy making music with Parvati. 'And in any case I'd only perform for a perfect audience.'

Narada rounded up Brahma and Vishnu, who hadn't seen Shiva's act for a while. So Shiva sang and before long, one by one, the damaged spirits recover from their disabilities. Shiva keeps singing, his voice reaching heights only accessible to gods. Vishnu melts with the beauty of it. Out of his toe a stream of water begins to flow.

It is the Ganges.

Those who had committed countless sins drank Ganges' water by the cartload, and felt the better for it. Extravagant and unsubstantiated claims were made for the spiritual power of this remarkable liquid. Merely to be touched by a breeze containing a drop of the Ganges erased the accumulated misbehaviour of many lifetimes, said one holy book. Another, the *Mahabhagavata-purana*, tells the story of a robber who, though sent to Hell after death, was subsequently elevated to Shiva's heaven because his flesh was eaten by a jackal who had drunk Ganges' water.

The Mughal emperors of India drank nothing else. In his *Ain-I-Akbari* (1610), Abul Fazl described Akbar the Great and his obsession:

> His Majesty calls this source of life 'the water of immortality', and has committed the care of this department to proper persons. He does not drink much, but pays much attention to this matter. Both at home and on travels he drinks the Ganges water. Some trustworthy persons are stationed on the banks of that river, who dispatch the water in sealed jars.

Although Muslims like Akbar did not share the Hindu belief in the river's divine origins, they prized the water for its other qualities: its sweetness, pleasant taste, and the absence of any smell or deterioration, despite its retention for any length of time. This provided convincing proof of its unusual character. The modern scientific explanation is that a low level of naturally occurring radiation in Ganges' water, while harmless to humans, kills or neutralises pathogens and bacteria.

I count myself fortunate that much of my childhood was spent beside a river I quickly came to know and love. In a futile and largely unsuccessful attempt to make a gentleman out of the unruly eight-year-old child that I was, my parents enrolled me in an elite boys boarding school, where I remained until I was sixteen.

The Southport School had extensive bush-covered grounds along the banks of the Nerang River, and in its crystal clear waters we learned to swim. Children who could swim a mile without stopping were awarded the title of King of the River, and permitted to adventure within limits but without supervision, in canoes and boats up and down the tidal estuary. It was a powerful incentive, and after a year of dedicated training, I succeeded.

Much of my inspiration at that time came from the writing of Mark Twain. *The Adventures of Huckleberry Finn* was on our school list of recommended reading. I read it obsessively. Huck Finn is a ten- or eleven-year-old boy who escapes from his abusive alcoholic father by faking his own violent death. He takes to the river in a canoe (and later, a raft) and lives on the Mississippi where his adventures and misadventures take place. The whole book is permeated by Twain's affectionate understanding of the great river of which he was so fond.

So it was in the rebellious spirit of Huck Finn that we defiantly explored the forbidden reaches of the

Nerang that were out of bounds to us as children. We fished and swam, stalked mud crabs among the mangroves and eels in limpid pools. Sometimes dolphins would find their way upriver gliding silently past, arching their backs in that wonderful sinuous rhythm that mimics the flow of water. Once a giant green sea turtle arrived, stayed a few days and left.

Whenever I felt lonely, lost or miserable, I'd borrow a canoe from a friend, paddle energetically as far as I could upstream and drift effortlessly back down with the current. And always I felt soothed and supported (as indeed I was) by the river that eventually became a surrogate parent and mentor. It was to the river that I confided my secrets, mourned my losses, expressed my desires and, like a loving friend, she silently but gently looked after me.

Fifty years later, with a book on the subject of water running behind time, I decided to rent a house-boat on the Manning River so that I could write in peace with the river for inspiration. I loaded the boat with food, tea, sake, research material, and set off upriver.

A Tang Dynasty poet described how he once slept in a wooden punt drifting on a lake of lotus flowers at night in order to absorb their energy or, as he put it, to 'dream the dreams of the lotus'. Alone in my boat I would, I hoped, dream the dreams of water that would illuminate my text. However, things didn't quite work out as I'd anticipated.

Three weeks later I returned happy, contented and peaceful. But I had written nothing, nothing at all. My days and nights had passed as if in a waking dream in which I absorbed from the river something more important than the writing of books. Whenever I felt guilty about not working I heard a voice, perhaps that of the sage Chang Tzu: 'the Tao that can be written is not the true Tao,' it said.

Or was this, I wondered, the voice of the river?

'You need do nothing,' it whispered.

I thought about the river people of South Africa, the *Abantubomlambo*, a race of half fish, half human beings, who live in deep pools at the bottom of fast flowing rivers. They have the power to 'call' humans, who are unable to resist. When someone hears the *Abantubomlambo*, say the Xhosa Bantu, they become restless and wander aimlessly about. Then suddenly they run to the river and plunge in, never to be seen again.

I wandered aimlessly about.

I explored narrow creeks and sheltered bays overhung with eucalypts, moving the boat only when the spirit moved me. Letting go of attachment to outcomes, rocking, anchored in the gentle current, watching white spoonbills delicately tiptoe through the reeds beside me, I became lost to the sensation of *being* with the river, of becoming one with its flow. Nights spent moored under stars shining in the deep blue of the sky, the calls of tawny frogmouth owls echoing across the water; sometimes, suddenly, a fish would jump. Sitting wrapped in a woven shawl on a deckchair on the roof, I played sixteenth-century cello CD's and drank warm sake in the light of the moon.

I re-read Conrad and Thoreau and Herman Hesse's *Siddartha*. Of all those who've written about water and spirit, Hesse is the one that moves me more than any other. In his twilight years Siddartha, still searching for peace, meets Vasudeva, a wise old man who ferries passengers across a river for a living. Siddartha decides to stay with him, to apprentice himself to this boatman, in order to learn the art of listening.

'You will learn it,' says Vasudeva 'but not from me. The river has taught me how to listen; you will learn from it too. The river knows everything; one can learn everything from it.'

Siddartha listens. Soon he begins to hear the many voices of the river. 'The voices of all living creatures are in its voice,' Vasudeva explains. Siddartha listens more, hears more, until one day he can no longer make distinctions and '. . . all the voices, all the goals, all the yearnings, all the sorrows, all the pleasures, all the good and evil, all of them together' become one.

'When Siddartha listened attentively to this river,' wrote Hesse, 'to this song of a thousand voices; when he did not listen to the sorrow or laughter, when he did not bind his soul to any one particular voice and absorb it in himself but heard them all, the whole, the unity; then the great song of a thousand voices consisted of one word; Om—perfection.'

The great song of a thousand voices . . . all we need to do is listen.

# The Way of the Waterfall

Waterfalls serve an important role in Buddhist
practice as symbols of impermanence and
supports for certain kinds of meditation.
Such places have a power that we cannot easily
describe or explain. When approached with an
awareness of the emptiness and luminosity
underlying all appearances they can encourage
us to expand our vision not only of ourselves but
of reality itself.

Tenzin Gyatso, The XIV Dalai Lama
of Tibet, 2004

In 1926 a party of tribal elders from the Sahara Desert was invited to visit Europe as guests of the French government. The aim of the exercise was to impress on these leaders the diversity and power of modern civilisation, particularly French civilisation, so that they would cease raiding French outposts and become good global citizens.

Of all the wonders the visitors encountered, the thing that made the most lasting impression was a waterfall. They were astonished to see vast quantities of the precious fluid pouring endlessly over a cliff. The neverending supply was the greatest of miracles; they could not believe that the source would not run dry. They waited a long while to see if it would peter out. Several days later they asked to return to the spot to see if it still flowed.

Waterfalls are dynamic expressions of power and energy. Massive falls such as the Victoria Falls on the Zambezi, the Iguazu in Brazil or the Niagara, draw us like magnets to witness the spectacle of their endless roar and mist-clad rainbows, and the mysteries they conceal.

The Kololo people who live near the great falls of the Zambezi River call them *musi ó tunya*, the smoke that thunders. In 1855, the missionary David Livingstone renamed them the Victoria Falls in honour of her Imperial Majesty. Livingstone concluded that the earth had been split open by an earthquake and the water of the Zambesi fell into this ready-made cleft. It certainly looks that way. Two kilometres (1.2 miles) wide and one hundred metres (328 feet) high, the Victoria Falls is the largest curtain of falling water in the world. The spray and mist can be seen from 30 kilometres (18 miles) away.

These falls were the home of the gods and ancestors of the Kololo. An anthropologist noted that they 'believe it is haunted by a malevolent and cruel divinity, and they make offerings to conciliate its favour'. An incessant roar fills the air with the sound of rolling thunder and the ground trembles and vibrates beneath one's feet. Double and treble rainbows bridge the chasm, forming a zone of prismatic colours of exceptional depth, brilliance and intensity. Under a full moon, a golden lunar rainbow emerges from the spray.

No wonder the locals thought it was the home of the gods.

Stories of gods and waterfalls form part of Japanese Buddhist practice and belief. Fudo the Immovable is a popular Buddhist deity in contemporary Japan. Encircled by flames engendered by the intensity of his concentration, Fudo holds in his right hand a *vajra* (ritual thunderbolt) sword to cut through the bonds of delusion. In his left is a rope lasso to drag reluctant sentient beings in the right direction.

Fudo is the patron saint of Shugendo, a fascinating seventh-century fusion of Buddhism, Shinto, Taoism and Tantra, whose practioners seek to accumulate wisdom and magic power by learning directly from nature and its indwelling spirit. Mountains, rivers and waterfalls are the universities where Shugendo, literally 'the way of the mountain ascetic', has its home. The wild-looking long-haired practitioners of its rigorous discipline are known as *Yamabushi*, 'those who sleep in the mountains'. With their magic formulas, charms and purification rituals, the Yamabushi have an impressive reputation as healers of mind and spirit. Much of this knowledge, they claim, is communicated directly to them by earth, stone and water.

The Nachi waterfall in the heavily forested mountains of Kumano is an object of particular veneration for the Yamabushi, and a national treasure for the rest of the nation. Here in the twelfth century the samurai warrior Mongaku undertook an extended session of 'cold water austerity', standing in the pool beneath the waterfall for 21 days reciting the Sanskrit mantra of Fudo, the Immovable.

*The Tale of Heike* (circa 1300) gives us some idea of just how cold it was:

> Deep snow lay upon the ground, and icicles
> hung thickly from the trees. The stream in the

ravine was silent. Freezing blasts swept down from the mountain tops. The waterfall's white threads were frozen into crystalline clusters and the trees were wrapped in white. Mongaku did not hesitate for an instant; he went down to the pool and waded in until the water reached his neck. Then he began to intone the invocation to Fudo-myo-o . . .

After eight days Mongaku collapsed but was revived by two helpful water spirits. When they reassured him that Fudo was listening intently to his prayers, Mongaku resumed his devotions with renewed stamina.

Shugendo adepts perform Mongaku's 'waterfall rite', standing in prayer for extended periods under the Nachi and other waterfalls. With a vertical drop of 133 metres (436 feet), Nachi is Japan's highest waterfall, and standing under it can be dangerous, especially after heavy rains. A recent visitor described the cascade as 'a raging white giant dancing tirelessly to the tune of the gods'.

Shinto scriptures use the word *kami* to identify any object, being or natural energy that exerts power over humans and their world. While *kami* have no perceptible form, waterfalls in particular are thought to be infused with spiritual and purifying energy. Bathing at night in cold rivers or standing in prayer beneath icy waterfalls are purification rituals that cleanse the soul and strengthen the spirit.

In 1835, when he was 74, the prolific Japanese genius Hokusai produced *A Tour of Japanese Waterfalls*, eight coloured woodblock prints that capture the beauty and diversity of falling water like no other works of art. The one hanging on my studio wall depicts a Zen master and two monks drinking sake high on a cliff overlooking the Amida Falls.

Long ago in a nearby shrine which is now *Chŏrŏ Jinta* (the Temple of the Long Waterfall), a monk named Dŏga, was lighting the sacred *Goma* fire, which symbolises the flames of wisdom consuming the wood of passion, when he saw reflected in a mirror the face of the Buddha Amida. Around this story has grown the belief that the Buddha is the incarnation of the *Kami* that inhabits the falls. Hence it is a popular desti-nation for Buddhist pilgrims and water-worshipping mountain ascetics.

Some aspire to an even more direct and intimate communion, to unite with the infinite energy of the waterfall itself. The ritual known as 'the abandonment of the body' is not suicide. It is the sacrifice of oneself out of a sense of compassion for, and the desire to benefit, all sentient beings. The Japanese call it *sokushin jobutsu*, 'to become Buddha in *this* body'.

On a bright summer's day in 1879, after one thousand days of fasting and deep meditation, the Shugendo master Gyo Ja Jitsukara clasped his palms together in an attitude of reverence, and jumped off the cliff into the arms of his beloved Nachi waterfall. It is said that when his body was found intact on the rocks at the bottom, it was still in the same devotional posture. The grave and shrine of Gyo Ja Jitsukara are holy places on the pilgrim path at Nachi. When I heard this story at a temple in Kyoto, I found it hard to understand such profound unity with the cosmos. 'It's just like your Jesus Christ,' a young Buddhist monk explained. 'He died on the cross for your sins and Gyo Ja Jitsukara died at Nachi for ours.'

Suddenly it all made sense.

Sadly, I didn't get to put flowers on Gyo Ja's grave at Nachi. I had fallen under the spell of another enchanted waterfall, the Sound of Feathers.

In 778 AD, Enchin, a Buddhist priest from Nara, had a vision in which he was told to 'look for the clear water origin of the Yodo River'. He followed the river through a thickly forested valley until he reached a mist-covered mountain where a waterfall poured out of the sheer rock face. Here Enchin built a small thatched hut and installed his hand-carved wooden image of the Bodhisattva Kannon.

The Sound of Feathers originates from a source deep inside Mount Otowa. It flows as it has always done, but Enchin's thatched hut has been replaced by a vast precinct of halls and shrines and pagodas known collectively as *Kiyomizudera*, the Clear Water Temple. The forest that surrounded it has become the city of Kyoto.

I had come a long way to listen to the Sound of Feathers. I wasn't the only one. This is one of the most revered water sources in Japan and its easy access assures its popularity. By 10 am, busloads of enthusiastic water worshippers were queueing patiently. Among them were hundreds of schoolchildren, mostly teenagers. 'This water will help us study better,' one told me, 'help us to concentrate our minds.'

The flow of the waterfall/spring is diverted into three carved marble channels that protrude from the tiled roof of a covered shrine set close to the mountain. Metal cups with 60 centimetre-long (2 foot) wooden handles sit in an ultraviolet light steriliser. I reach in, take one, and join the crowd holding out their cups to receive the water's blessing. When mine is full, I drink it slowly and give thanks to the spring. The taste still lingers in my memory even now.

Next morning at 5 am I am back at the Sound of Feathers. I set up my camera and wait. Soon, a barefoot young man in the knee-length white tunic of the Yamabushi materialises out of the mist and stands under one of the spouts, his palms together in prayer. He stays for half an hour.

Later, a well-dressed older man arrives with two empty Evian bottles and fills them one by one in the falling stream.

'I come every day for my water,' he said in English.

'What does it do for you?' I asked.

'It keeps me young,' he smiled as he waved goodbye.

It didn't occur to me to ask how old he was. He might have been a young-looking 90. Perhaps this was the Fountain of Youth. That morning, with the dawn chorus of the birds echoing through the mist-shrouded mountain temple, it all seemed possible.

Once, when the Norse troublemaker Loki had offended the gods of Asgard, he fled from their wrath to the mountains where he built a cabin with four doors so that he could see in all directions. During the day he transformed himself into a salmon and hid in the pool below the Franang Waterfall. At night he emerged to sit by the fire knitting fishing nets from twine.

When Odin, Thor and the rest of the posse approached the cabin, Loki threw his half-finished net into the fire, reverted to his salmon incarnation and leaped into the pool. Recovering the charred remains of the net, the gods realised that this was a clever device for catching fish. So they made their own and tried to catch Loki who managed to evade capture until, cornered, he leaped over the net and was caught by Thor who managed to grab him by the tail. That's why salmon have a tapering tail—it was compressed by the thunder god's powerful grip.

If Loki had been a real salmon he would have made his getaway by jumping *up* the waterfall. How fish actually do this has never been satisfactorily explained. It's a familiar sight on nature documentaries—trout and salmon leaping progressively up waterfalls till they reach the top. A close examination of this footage shows that fish half way up high waterfalls continue to project themselves to the next level in a series of jumps. But how can they jump when they're still in mid-air?

What do they know that we don't?

The deep pools and potholes at the base of waterfalls are thought by some Africans to be the home of ghosts, spirits of the dead who sometimes emerge to steal sheep or goats grazing nearby. People too are at risk. One way of escaping from the clutches of the waterfall demons is to cut yourself slightly because they only take unblemished victims.

Europeans believed that the souls of the departed, released from the womb of Mother Earth in the bodies of fish, migrated upstream through rivers and streams to the springs at the source, where they were resurrected and ascended to their heavenly home. People who drowned were victims of these water-dwelling spirits. The spectacle of millions of fish swimming effortlessly upstream against a current powerful enough to sweep all before it, was an annual reminder of this mystery.

Viktor Schauberger, a meticulous observer of nature and water, was intrigued by this ability of trout to overcome their own weight and the pressure of water flowing against them. Some of the waterfalls they climbed were 60 metres (180 feet) high. If he could discover the mechanism by which they were able to do this, Schauberger reasoned, then perhaps it might be possible to design a machine that could overcome the force of gravity.

On a moonlit night when the pond at the base of a high fall teemed with migrating fish, Schauberger sat and watched a large trout arrive at the point where the water fell onto the surface of the pond. The fish seemed to rock to and fro 'in strongly pronounced looping movements' as if it were dancing a reel. Then it dived down and returned to the spot beneath the falls.

Schauberger describes what happened next: 'The trout suddenly stood up on its tail and in the conically converging stream of water I perceived a wild movement like a spinning top . . . Having temporarily disappeared, the trout then re-emerged from this spinning movement and floated motionlessly upwards. Upon reaching the underside of the topmost curve of the waterfall it did a quick somersault in a high curve upstream (backwards like that of the child) and with a loud smack was thrown beyond the upper curvature. With a powerful flick of its tail-fins it disappeared.'

Is some natural or supernatural energy responsible for this inexplicable gymnastic performance?

Behind the waterfall where I go for my neck and shoulder massage is a well-trodden path to a spot where I sit and dream of those who have been there before me. It's filled with the energy of the water singing and dancing in front of you. That space which lies behind the waterfall may sometimes be filled with marvels.

The sixteenth-century Chinese allegorical epic, *Monkey*, begins with the following story: One day, some forest monkeys playing by a stream realised that none of them knew where the water came from, so they decided to follow it to its source. Scrambling up the steep mountain slope they eventually reached the source, a great waterfall. Standing before the cascade, they said to one another: 'If anyone is bold enough to pierce this curtain, get to where the water has its origins and return unharmed, we will make him our king.'

'I will go,' announces Monkey, ever the fearless hero.

Crouching, he screws up his eyes and jumps straight through the waterfall. But there is no water there. Instead, there's an iron bridge, with a stream flowing below it. Crossing the bridge, Monkey finds a wonderful illuminated cavern furnished with furniture and crockery made from crystal. An inscription carved into the rock face reads 'This Cave of the Water Curtain in the blessed land of the Mountain of Flowers and Fruit leads to Heaven.' Jumping back outside, Monkey takes the others through to the cave and, after some persuasion, they make him their king.

The oral traditions of the New York Iroquois tell us that He-no, the Spirit of Thunder, once dwelt behind the Niagara Falls. His voice was the roaring of the waters. There is an oft-repeated tale that every year the Iroquois used to sacrifice a woman, sending her over the falls in a birch bark canoe, but the indigenous story is that one of He-no's half-human assistants fell in love with a beautiful Indian girl and took her back to live with him. Eventually she was transformed into a water sprite, dancing in the spray of the lunar rainbow. However, when the storm spirits started fighting one another in the sky, He-no was sent to restore order. From that time on he and his extended family dwelt among the clouds keeping the peace.

He-no sometimes comes to earth in human form dressed as a warrior. In his hair he wears a magic feather which protects him from malevolent forces. On one of these visits He-no confronted a demonic serpent that terrified the Iroquois. Every spring, when the rivers were loosing themselves from the frozen grip of winter and pouring their water into Lake Erie, the creature would emerge from its cave near the falls. Hungry after its long hibernation the serpent would visit the burial grounds on dark moonless nights to feed on the bodies of the dead. In its wake it left a sinuous trail of poison and disease that killed many people.

He-no pursued the monster relentlessly until he caught up with it at Buffalo Creek and crippled it with a bolt of lightening. Thrashing around in agony the serpent pushed the banks of the creek into winding bends that remain to this day. As the dying monster was swept down the Niagara River to the edge of the great cataract it arched backwards in a semicircle extending from one side to the other. The dead body restrained the water for a while but when it carved a passage through the ledge which shelved out over the abyss, The Horse Shoe Falls came into being.

Nature-worshipping cultures tapped into the spiritual energy of waterfalls in several ways. Behind the water curtain of some Scandinavian cascades live spirits who teach music. Näkki, the unpredictable water spirit of Finland, has been known to seize people and animals who bathe in the sea or swim in his rivers; for entertainment he plays the violin, and occasionally passes on this gift to humans at waterfalls.

Timing is important. On Midsummer Night, or the days preceding Lent and Easter, the spirit may appear on a rock surrounded by water below a waterfall. The intending pupil must bring a violin and sit on this rock and wait. When Näkki emerges from the curtain of the falls he will seat himself on the same rock, with his back turned to the aspiring virtuoso, and begin the tuition.

Here's the tricky part.

During the lesson the pupil must bind himself with a rope to the waist of his spirit master, but not too firmly. The knots should come undone easily if, or when, the spirit should suddenly dive sideways into the water. 'If the fetters do not loosen,' the story warns, 'the pupil falls under the power of the Water Spirit.' Those who survive this learning process become great masters who can make people dance against their will. The violin he or she plays may continue to produce haunting melodies on its own. This is the mythic origin of much of the folk music of Scandinavia—communicated to humans by the spirit of the waterfall.

Throughout the literature of waterfalls, the lure of the abyss, beautiful women and the threat of enchantment are constantly recurring themes.

In his psychic thriller, *The Hasheesh Eater* (1857), Fitz Hugh Ludlow's depressed hero encounters an attractive woman beside the Niagara Falls while he's feeling 'helpless, friendless, frequently deserted utterly of every human being'. She turns out to be a demonic fiend who encourages him to jump—but he pulls back just in time. Dropping her human disguise she gives a hollow laugh. 'I would have to cast you to the fishes,' she whispers intimately in his ear.

On the banks of the Rhine, farmers tell stories about Princess Ilse, the captivating daughter of the Giant of the Ilsenstein. Many giants, knights and princes competed for the honour of sharing their worldly goods (and their bed) with the fairy princess, but she was in love with the handsome Lord Westerburg who lived nearby. Her father thought that consorting with a mere mortal was bringing shame on the giant family. He forbade her to see her lover, but she paid no heed. The Castle of Westerburg became a home away from home.

One day when Ilse threatened to leave home for good, the exasperated giant lost control. Stretching out his huge hands he tore a great rift between his castle on the heights and Westerburg below. Looking down from the cleft filled with rushing water that separated her from her lover, Princess Ilse threw herself over the falls and became a nymph. She lives in the pool at the base of the cascade, appearing sometimes to invite mortals to join her. The Emperor Henry visited her pools frequently, waiting for a vision of her white arms waving to entice him into the cool spray.

We are attracted to waterfalls because there's something in the air. And there is indeed. The energy of moving water generates negative ions, neg-ions. When water breaks up, the positive electrical charge remains with the larger drop while the negative charge is dispersed with the spray, forming neg-ions. The same thing happens at the seashore. Neg-ions make us feel good; they promote and intensify a sense of well-being, which might explain why Niagara Falls has been a mecca for honeymooning couples since 1810.

'Pity that virgin soul on passion's brink,' wrote the poet Richard Watson Guilder in 1894, unable to resist the cliché-ridden metaphor of innocent water on the edge of the unknown. 'Cruel as love and wild as love's first kiss. Oh god! the abyss.'

Oscar Wilde was not impressed with the abyss or the falls above it. Brought by his hosts to admire the spectacle, Wilde wrote: 'Every American bride is taken here, and the sight of the stupendous waterfall must be one of the earliest, if not the keenest, disappointments in American married life.'

Francis Abbott fell in love. Arriving at Niagara Falls in June 1829 intending to stay only a few days, he never left. Renting a cabin near the edge of the falls Francis spent his time in contemplation. 'In the wildest hours of the night,' wrote a neighbour in a letter, he was often seen 'walking alone and undismayed in the most dangerous places near the Falls.'

Soon 'the Hermit of the Falls' became a legend.

In the early to mid-nineteenth century hermits were status symbols for those who had everything. Fashionable British gentry employed full-time hermits in tattered robes to live in landscaped grottos near equally artificial fountains and waterfalls on their baronial estates. But the Hermit of the Falls was the real thing. Stories of his stoic disinterest in his own mortality fascinated the growing crowd of interested spectators, as did his habit of bathing in the icy river on winter days. Cold water austerity, meditation, and withdrawal from society—was Francis Abbott consciously or unconsciously following in the path of the Yamabushi?

In 1831, two years after he came to Niagara, Francis did not return from his regular morning dip. His body was found floating at the base of the falls. Did he suicide or was his two-year stay a preparation for his final act of *sokushin jobutsu*? Before he left his cabin that day Francis destroyed his journals and other writings, so we will never know.

Would-be suicides, defiant daredevils, devout water worshippers, excited honeymooners—Niagara welcomed them all. Some went over the falls in barrels and didn't come back. Others rode bicycles across tightropes. In 1957, a man claiming to be God attempted to prove it by walking on the water in front of his 'disciples'. They went away disillusioned when he was swept to his death.

Even people who had no interest in prematurely leaving this vale of tears were mesmerised by the power, energy and spirituality of the falls. Harriet Beecher-Stowe, author of *Uncle Tom's Cabin*, felt this during her holiday at Niagara in 1834. 'It would have been a beautiful death,' she wrote wistfully.

What is it about Niagara that makes it the most popular suicide venue in North America? Is it because it epitomises the endless cycle of birth, death and rebirth, of consciousness emerging from nothingness and returning to nothingness?

Dr Moses Blaine, a Niagara Falls physician between 1879 and 1905, remarked on the 'uncanny' effect of the falls on some people. He called the condition, *hydracropsychic*. It rendered 'even the will of the active robust man in the prime of life temporarily invalid, as if under the spell of a malevolent hypnotist'. 'Such a one,' he continued, 'drawn to the rapids above the Falls, may stand for long minutes staring as if paralysed. Speak to him in the most forcible tone, he will not hear you. Touch him, or attempt to restrain him, he may throw off your hand angrily.' The root cause of this, Doctor Blaine suggested, was 'a mysterious biological attraction to the thunderous force of nature represented by the Falls'.

This mysterious magnetic power of nature is not so much biological as spiritual. We are drawn to waterfalls and seashores to reflect on our origins and our ultimate destination.

We come from water, we are sustained by water and to water we will eventually return. This is the mantra I intone when I sit beneath the unnamed cascade in the forest not far from my house. Its fall is high enough and light enough to massage neck, back, arms and head. All I need to do is position myself appropriately and the water does the rest. That's why water's called the Black Masseur.

There is a Qigong visualisation in which you imagine yourself under a waterfall that progressively washes away the outer layers of dirt, then deeply circulates through the body, cleansing physical, emotional and spiritual impurities. This is, literally, absolution—purification and rebirth, immersing oneself in the Divine. In a passage from *North America* (1862), the English novelist Anthony Trollope evokes this sense of unity and identity with the movement of the waters:

> To realise Niagara, you must sit there till you see nothing else than that which you have come to see. You will hear nothing else. At length you will be at one with the tumbling river before you. You will find yourself among the waters as though you belonged to them. The cool liquid green will run through your veins and the voice of the cataract will be the expression of your own heart. You will fall as the bright waters fall, rushing down into your new world with no hesitation and no dismay; and you will rise again as the spray rises, bright, beautiful and pure. Then you will flow away in your course to the uncompassed, distant and eternal ocean.

Such is the way of the waterfall, of all waterfalls.

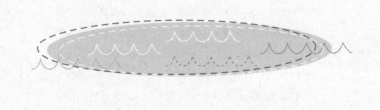

# The Lake of Imagination

In each of us lies this dark lake from which our
conscious reasoning selves have gradually
emerged...Some of us love to dream on the banks
of this mysterious mere; some try to fish or dive in
it; others labour to brick it over and blot it out.

Frank Laurence Lucas
*The Decline and Fall of the
Romantic Ideal*, 1930

When Marco Polo visited Hangchow in the thirteenth century, he was amazed at its beauty and sophistication. Of all the cities he'd seen, this, he said, was the 'most splendid'. A highlight of his tour was a boat trip on the West Lake, which in his opinion 'offered more refreshment and delectation than any other experience on earth'. This was high praise indeed from someone who'd seen so many wonderful things.

West Lake is the origin and focus of many ancient folktales and legends. A ten-volume anthology of these, published in 1986, reveals the importance of this body of water in Chinese art, architecture, history and garden design. Not far from the lake's shores are historic sites such as the Jade Spring, the Tiger Spring, the Dragon Well, the Yellow Dragon Cave and the shrine known as Autumn Moon on Calm Lake.

Narrow causeways divide the lake, creating reflections on either side as you walk along. There is no edge or border, so the causeways with their green willows and flowering pink peach blossoms seem to float on the still mirror of the water. With its exquisite villas and gardens, temples and monasteries, West Lake has been a source of inspiration for Chinese artists, poets and contemplatives for millennia; and you can still sit by its shore, sipping fragrant tea made with water from the Jade Spring while you wait for the moon to rise. Here the Taoist poet Saikodan wrote:

The shadow of the bamboo sweeps the steps,
But the dust does not stir.
The moon's disc bores into the lake
But the water shows no scars.

Meditating on the changing moods of sky and clouds, sun, moon and stars reflected in a great liquid looking-glass allows us access to depths of consciousness previously hidden. A sense of peace, tranquillity and unity with the cosmos overcomes the more familiar imperative of everyday urgency. And the longer you stay beside a lake the more tranquil your spirit becomes.

'I am certain,' W.B. Yeats wrote in 1893, 'that the water, the water of the seas and of lakes and of mist and rain, has all but made us after its image. Images form themselves in our minds perpetually as if they were reflected in some pool . . . We can make our minds so still like water that beings gather about us that they may see their own images and so live for a moment with a clearer, perhaps even with a fiercer life because of our quiet. Did not the wise Porphyry think that all souls come to be born because of water, and that "even the generation of images in the mind is from water?" '

Stillness of mind has been compared to a calm lake—one without ripples. When a lake is in this state everything on the bottom can be seen. When the wind creates ripples nothing is visible. The still lake is an evocative image of the mind at rest and, as it communicates itself to us, we too are drawn towards a sense of peace within our turbulent selves.

My main diet while writing in my cabin beside the lake at Mallacoota was fresh fish caught with an illegal 15 metres (50 foot) net put out not far from shore among the sea grasses. It had to be taken in by sunrise. Detection meant a fine and confiscation. The Fisheries inspector started work at 7.30 am and he took his job very seriously. Not only that, we were quite good friends. So for all those reasons I took no chances.

The lake fed me royally. Sole, whiting, bream, blackfish, mullet and flathead, all appeared on the menu at one time or another. Once there were twelve flathead waiting patiently to be hauled on board. I fried their livers with onions and a little garlic, and froze the fillets for the following week. Then one day a terrible thing happened. As I slowly drew in the net, folding it carefully in the bottom of the dinghy, I could see deep down a large flash of silver rising towards the surface. It was an old man of the lake, a jewfish so heavy that I couldn't lift it into the boat. He had been dead for several hours.

Overcome with awe and remorse, I rowed back to the jetty towing him behind me. I manhandled the great body onto the waterside bench set aside for cleaning fish and I sat beside him thinking. How was I going to deal with this? The venerable fish was dead and I was responsible. Looking into his eyes I asked his spirit for forgiveness, and thanked him for the gift of himself. Then I scaled and cleaned the carcass and cut it into meal size steaks. A few bloodstained scales stuck to my trousers, each a third of the size of my hand. Washed, they resembled fine rainbow-tinted perspex lenses. I kept them on my desk. The colours soon faded but they retained their significance.

Later that same week, in an obscure anthropological text, I came across an indigenous North American lake story about the magical scales of a giant silver fish. Was this a message from an invisible mentor or was it coincidence? Either way it made my mementos even more precious.

Here is the story.

When the Great Spirit of the Iroquois was adorning the world with beauty, he scooped a deep hollow from a rocky mountain and set therein a wonderful lake nourished by rich streams whose virgin waters sent their most precious offerings. The guardian was Ga-ye-was, a mighty fish who could assume mortal form whenever he wished to visit the lands surrounding his domain. But Ga-ye-was was not happy. His life was a lonely one with no partner to share his waterbed.

One day as Ga-ye-was was floating and singing on the lake he saw a graceful Indian girl listening as the waves carried his song to shore. Her name was Gi-da-no-neh. Gi-da-no-neh's life was not a happy one either. Her parents had promised her to an old man whose feet were too slow for the hunt, his spirit too still for war. Warmth had departed from his heart and in his lodge there was little joy. Gi-da-no-neh was young and the promise of the world lay bright before her. So far she had managed to keep her elderly suitor at bay, but the time of union was fast approaching. Her troubled heart sought solace on the shores of the lake where every sunset she came to listen to the song of the waters, which seemed to grow stronger and more vibrant the longer she remained.

Retracing her steps one evening, Gi-da-no-neh found on the forest path beside the lake two extra-ordinary fish. Around them in a circle were rare geometric silver brooches of fine workmanship much prized by the Iroquois. They glowed with the reflected fire of the sunset.

Had someone followed her? The girl looked around. There was no-one. All was still. She gathered the shining brooches and fastened them to her faded doeskin tunic. Gi-da-no-neh felt so beautifully adorned that she shivered with pride and pleasure.

Then there were the two strange fish. She made a fire to roast them and had begun to eat when her father arrived looking for her. He stared at the brooches on her clothing. Who had given them to her? Gi-da-no-neh would not answer. Surely some evil spirit was trying to tempt the girl. Fearful and angry, he tore the brooches from her dress, threw them in the lake and followed his daughter, weeping for her lost treasures, back to their lodge. Her mother and father forbade Gi-da-no-neh to return to the lake. 'It is dangerous for you', they said.

But every sunset she felt the lake calling, waiting. At last she could no longer resist. The fish she had eaten had made her so thirsty, and the water of the spring that trickled out of a mound near the lodge tasted progressively more bitter with each passing day. Only the sweet water of the lake could quench this unnatural thirst.

So one afternoon as the sun was going down, Gi-da-no-neh ran away from her people and did not stop until she reached the lake. Wading in until the water was up to her knees she drank deeply, sighing with relief. Suddenly she felt as if the bottom was giving way beneath her. She closed her eyes. As two strong arms grasped her firmly she heard a familiar voice as musical as a running brook say 'Have no fear Gi-da-no-neh, I am Ga-ye-was, your devoted lover'.

Her eyes opened wide with surprise, pleasure and disbelief. Holding her close was the tall young warrior of imposing demeanour who sometimes appeared in her dreams. He told her of his long-standing infatuation; how he waited for her each sunset, how he had sung to her and her alone, how the power of his charm song had drawn her back to the lake. Having eaten the magic fish, he said, she could never be content to live on land but would always thirst for his water.

And the brooches that she loved so much he offered to replace, and more. For they were the scales of the cloak he wore in his fish incarnation. As his woman she too would have a covering of silver. Would she be his companion forever, he asked? Settling herself into the warmth of his embrace Gi-da-no-neh did not even need to think about her answer.

When the sun was high in the sky on the following day, her troubled father, who had been wandering around the lake all night, heard her voice. 'Hear me, father,' she called, as the waters parted to reveal the lovers in each other's arms. 'You loved me truly but you did not know my heart. My lover rules these waves and I have pledged myself to him. I shall return no more to my life on the land. You will never see me again. And so farewell.' As the waters closed over the couple, the anguished parent heard an eerie melody— two voices singing, echoing in the stillness.

So when an Iroquois fisherman catches a fish of unusual beauty and size he retells the story, saying 'This is a true child of Ga-ye-was, the fish chief and his Indian wife, Gi-da-no-neh'.

Perhaps my ancient jewfish was the product of such a union. I feasted on his flesh with reverence, absorbing as much as I could of his power and wisdom.

Often before sunrise I'd wake, dress warmly and walk through the scented pine forest to a promontory overlooking the lake. From the mist-shrouded shoreline the haunting plaintive high-pitched calls of wild swans rose above the murmur of ducks and the screams of waterfowl. I remembered how Socrates waiting for his death draught of hemlock, had turned to Plato saying that 'swans sing more merrily at the approach of death because of the joy they have in going to the gods they serve'.

Swans, and the gods they serve, inhabit both the lakes of imagination and reality. The white swan is the symbol of the transmigrating soul. Celtic votive cauldrons found in sacred lakes (circa 600 BC) show cult wagons drawn by swans. The white swan is the avatar of Shiva and the Norse Valkyries, the vehicle of the Greek sun god Helios and the symbol of the Great Spirit of the North American peoples.

Cambodian scriptures speak of the snow-white swan as the living manifestation of light itself, and of the divine swans that swim on the 'lake of the heart' of the yoga adept. A realised Hindu Yogi master is referred to reverently as a *paramahamsa* or 'supreme swan', one who has liberated himself from the bondage of the phenomenal sphere.

The Buryat people on the shores of Siberia's Lake Baikal tell their children the archetypal story of the hunter who sees three beautiful maidens swimming nude in the lake. Hanging on a nearby bush are three white swan feather cloaks. Quietly, he reaches for one of the magnificent robes and stows it in his sack. Then when the young women return only two transform themselves back into swans and fly away.

The third remained naked and helpless and, as in many swan maiden legends, became the wife of the hunter who locked her costume safely in an old chest. After giving birth to 17 children, the swan wife finds the key, opens the trunk, wraps her magic cloak around her and prepares to join her feathered friends. Before leaving, she has a few last words with her distraught husband. 'I come from the skies,' she says, 'and to the skies I must now return. Every year in spring when you see us flying north, you must celebrate our passing with special rites.' Ceremonies welcoming the annual migration of the swans are still performed in Siberian villages today.

Their principal destination, the inspiration for Tchaikovsky's evocative ballet, *Swan Lake*, is Lake Baikal, the Blue Pearl of Siberia, the oldest, deepest and most remarkable lake on Earth. 'The Blue Pearl' contains one-fifth of the world's fresh water in its mile-deep basin. High in oxygen and low in mineral content, the purity of Baikal's water is maintained by a unique ecosystem in which a tiny industrious shrimp called *epishura* filters out algae and bacteria, while other minute scavengers reduce larger particles of organic matter. Of the 2500 species and sub-species that live in and around Baikal, 70 per cent survive nowhere else.

'Ordinary' lakes have a maximum lifespan of around 50,000 years, but they usually fill with silt, evaporate and disappear long before that. Lake Baikal is two million years old. Its hydrothermal vents support rich communities of unique subterranean life. While most large bodies of still water become stratified, Baikal has tides similar to those of the ocean, which promote deep oxygen circulation, ensuring uniform water quality from top to bottom. The lake is fed by a powerful spring of fresh water and 336 streams, each with a separate indwelling spirit, with its own individual character. Only one, the Angara, flows out.

Once upon a time, it seems that 'old man' Baikal had 337 daughters, obedient, well-behaved and quite happy to stay at home to help with the daily chores. Only one, Angara, became increasingly rebellious. She yearned to explore the wide open spaces of the *Taiga*. A friendly swan had told her stories of Yenisei, the wild warrior river of the west, and Angara longed to mingle her waters with his.

One night while the family were sleeping, Angara burst forth, carving a deep cleft in the mountain barrier that separated her from her destiny. The noise woke her father who threw a massive granite boulder to try to block her path. But it was useless. Angara flowed around the obstacle and off to meet Yenisei. United, the two lovers flowed onward to the sea.

The great boulder, known as Shaman Rock, remains in mid-stream. It became a place of judgement and divination where shamans would go to worship Burkhan, the spirit of the lake. In the hallowed presence of 'the invincible white god' only the truth must be spoken. If a man accused of a crime asserted his innocence, then he was taken by boat to the rock and left there overnight. Many died of fright. If the person survived physically and emotionally until morning he would be welcomed back into the community.

Apparently Burkhan was easily insulted and did not take kindly to being referred to as a lake. In his *Notes on the Russian Embassy to China, 1692–1695*, Everest

Ides pointed out that before he sailed, 'many people warned me with great fervour and begged me when I ventured out onto that ferocious sea not to call it a lake but a *dalay* or sea. They added that a great many distinguished people who headed out onto Baikal and called it a lake, that is, stagnant water, quickly fell victim to violent storms and ended up in mortal danger.'

The lakes of Tibet are also deep repositories of spirit. Fossilised seashells and marine creatures can be found on their shores, reminders that forty million years ago this country was at the bottom of the sea. Then a massive geological upheaval thrust the Himalayas and the basin of Tibet up into its present lofty altitude.

Himalayan myths and scriptures tell of a time when Tibet was one great lake of which the existing lakes are mere remnants. The famous Blue Lake of A-mdo has a circumference of 300 kilometres (186 miles). Wild storms sweep across the surface until it ices over in November. Long ago, the story goes, the bed of the lake was one vast plain; at its centre was a spring. Nearby lived an old woman who sent her daughter to fetch water daily from the spring. Because this was a magic spring, she warned the youngster never to forget to replace the large flat stone that covered it. But one day the inevitable happened. The girl forgot. The water kept on flowing and flooded 10,000 homes. Malevolent springs overflowing to inundate

the surrounding countryside is such a common explanation for the origin of lakes in many cultures that it
must be linked to actual floods that have occurred,
perhaps as a result of earthquakes in the past.

Of the Tibetan lakes, Manasarovar is the one most
liberally endowed with religious and mythological
associations. It lies near the snow-capped peak of
Mount Kailas, the Navel of the Earth. Kailas is Asia's
sacred mountain. Pilgrims from four different faiths
come to pay homage to the 6,000 metre (22,000 foot)
pyramid of rock known as the Throne of the Gods. To
the followers of Bonpo, the pre-Buddhist nature-
worshipping religion of Tibet and Mongolia, Kailas is
the 'Nine Storey Swastika Mountain'. And indeed on
the southern face, a vertical gully intersects with horizontal striations in the rock to create a massive natural
swastika—the 3000-year-old symbol of spiritual
attainment.

Twenty-nine kilometres (18 miles) south, reflecting
the towering male energy of Kailas, is its inseparable
female equivalent, Lake Manasarovar. The union of holy
lake and mountain represent the supreme duality of god
and goddess, yin and yang, height and depth, activity
and receptivity. Both have been loved and venerated by
countless generations of Jains, Hindus, Buddhists and
Bonpos as long as anyone can remember.

Each religion has its own story.

On the eve of the birth of Buddha, his mother Queen Maya dreamed that an assembly of gods accompanied her to Anotatta, the mysterious lake of ancient legends. Here she bathed to cleanse herself of impurities. When her womb was ready to receive the holy spirit, Maya saw the baby Buddha riding towards her on the back of a white elephant and, behind him in the distance, was the resplendent white peak of Mount Kailas. Because of Queen Maya's dream, some Buddhists identify Manasarovar as the earthly manifestation of Lake Anottata. Others say that this was where Buddha addressed 500 *Bodhisattvas*, each sitting on a separate lotus flower in the middle of the lake.

Hindu scriptures identify Mount Kailas as the home of Lord Brahma, the Creator God from whose mind the lake emanated. In the pre-Vedic Dreamtime, 12 wise Rishis retreated to Kailas to fast, meditate and practise austerities. But there was a problem—there was no water anywhere for miles, no water to drink or to bathe in. And without water, they could not perform the essential purification rituals.

The Rishis appealed to Brahma for help. Out of the depths of his unfathomable mind, Brahma brought forth a lake filled with water of great purity and infused with healing power. As the Rishis knelt down before it a giant glowing lingam (phallus) slowly rose out of the waves. They called the lake

Manasarovar, the Mind ('*manas*' from Sanscrit) of Brahma. Here, according to the *Ramayana*, one may find the key to Paradise:

> When the earth of Manasarovar touches anyone's body, or when anyone bathes in the lake, he shall go to the Paradise of Brahma, and he who drinks its waters shall go to the heaven of Shiva and shall be released from the sins of a hundred births. Even the beast who bears the name of Manasarovar shall go to the Paradise of Brahma. Its waters are like pearls.

This is truly a holy place, sanctified by centuries of devotion, where nature and divinity unite in a landscape of great beauty and spiritual *mana*.

While some lakes are filled with spirit, others are the home of ancient creatures who sometimes interact with humans. At five in the morning, Kiem Lake in the centre of Hanoi hums with activity—thousands of pre-dawn joggers in tracksuits, enthusiastic groups of Tai Chi exponents, old men walking in white singlets. As I walked around the tree-lined circuit I noticed a large group at the southern end. When I came closer an excited young Vietnamese boy approached me, took my hand and led me through the dense crowd, gently pushing people aside in his urgency until we reached the low stone wall that borders the lake.

A light mist hung suspended. Everyone was still, silent, looking intently at the dark water. The sun had not yet risen. I looked down at the boy, who pointed to a spot where a willow's fronds trailed. There was nothing there. Suddenly a giant antediluvian head rose to the surface, opened its huge mouth and disappeared into the depths once more. The reverence of the people was contagious. Had they been Christians they would probably have fallen to their knees and turned their eyes towards the heavens.

As it was we remained focused on the water, silently waiting for another glimpse of the marvellous creature. The father of my young guide joined us. 'You are very lucky to see the turtle god,' he said. 'It is a rare thing. They say he is older than five hundred years. This is the first time I have seen him and I come here often. It is a . . .' he stopped in mid-sentence as the giant turtle surfaced again, this time very close to us. For a few breathless seconds we looked into its five hundred-year-old eyes. The massive shell was encrusted with weeds and small molluscs. Then it inhaled loudly and vanished.

We waited in silence. How long I do not know. We did not notice the sun rise or hear the deafening song of the thousands of birds in the trees or the distant roar of motorcycle traffic. Time stood still. But the turtle god of Kiem Lake had gone. I shook hands with the boy and his father and thanked them.

Later that morning in a temple on an island in the lake, surrounded by candles and incense, I stood before the preserved remains of the mate of the giant turtle. Once there had been two of them. Being a god can be a lonely business. I felt sad for him.

The *Geography of Annam* tells how King Thai-To of the Le Dynasty, sailing on Kiem Lake, encountered an enormous tortoise which swam towards him. The frightened king drew his jewelled sword to strike the animal but the tortoise seized the weapon in its powerful jaws and dived to the bottom of the lake. The sword was not seen again until 1418 AD when Vietnam was occupied by the Chinese. A young fisherman, Le-Loi, cast his net into the lake and brought out a jewelled sword 'which flashed out rays of lightning when he took it in his hand'. Inspired, Le-Loi led a ten-year battle for independence (1418–1428), expelled the invaders and was crowned king in Hanoi.

Before his coronation, Le-Loi returned to make an offering and give thanks to the lake spirit. The king-to-be arrived in state, 'girt with his magic sword and escorted by an enormous crowd going before and behind; but he had scarcely reached the borders of the mere when there was a noise like a clap of thunder, whereupon the entire assemblage saw Le-Loi's sword leap from its scabbard transformed into a jade-coloured dragon which plunged into the waters and disappeared'.

The lake spirit had itself become the sword in order to defeat the Chinese. Hence the lake became known as Hoan-kiem-ho—'the Lake of the Long Sword'—in honour of this miracle. Hearing this story I understood the people's reverence and love for the ancient creature, and how privileged I was to have a brief connection with it.

What is it about lakes and swords, I wondered, thinking of the magic sword Excalibur, given to King Arthur by Viviane, the white-robed Lady of the Lake.

The Lady of the Lake was a prophetess, a water spirit with oracular powers who lived in an under-water palace in the lake that surrounds the Isle of Avalon. Arthurian folklore has it that after Arthur's first sword was broken in battle, the wizard Merlin told him that an unbreakable sword was to be found in a lake nearby. When they got there they saw, in the middle of the lake, a woman's arm 'clothed in white samite, mystic, wonderful' holding aloft a long gleaming sword. Arthur rowed out in a boat and took the sword from the hand of the patient underwater sprite who had been holding it up for hours.

The original name of the magic sword was Calad-Bolg, Gaelic for 'hard lightning'. French writers of

Arthurian epics found Calad-Bolg impossibly clumsy and after a few transitional names it finally became Excalibur.

When Arthur was mortally wounded, he asked Sir Bedivere to return Excalibur to the lake. When Bedivere threw it into the water, the white-robed arm emerged once more, a spirit hand grasped the hilt and waved it three times in farewell before disappearing forever.

The Lady of the Lake is the spiritual sister of the Celtic water goddess Coventina to whom offerings of weapons were often made. Most surviving examples of Celtic metal craftsmanship have been fished out of lakes and rivers where they were consigned as votive offerings. The conquering Romans were well aware of this custom. When the legions invaded the territory of the Vocae Tectosages, a tribe of famous lake worshippers in southern Gaul, the victorious commander sold the lakes by public auction to enthusiastic treasure hunters. The Roman historian Strabo wrote of the Celts that, 'lakes, in particular, provided inviolability for their treasures', which included exquisite jewellery and hand wrought caldrons. At Lake Neuchâtel in Switzerland around 100 BC, the Celts built a special wooden platform from which they cast their offerings into the water. Among the Celtic weapons recovered from the site were 270 spears, 27 shields and 170 swords. Similar lake shrines have been found in the British Isles and other centres of Celtic culture.

The worship of lake spirits began with the lake dwellers, prehistoric people, who lived in huts on timber platforms supported by tall piles. Wooden walkways connected the villages to shore. After the accidental discovery of a submerged village in Lake Zurich in 1853, remains of similar settlements were discovered in lakes throughout Europe and Britain.

When their descendants left the lakes to become farmers on dry land, the traditions, beliefs and customs of the lake dwellers were retained. The lake was their place of origin: the singing swans, divine manifestations of the goddess. Eventually the remains of these Palaeolithic villages became the legendary 'cities' of the Other World whose ruins could sometimes be glimpsed deep below the surface of the water, providing irrefutable evidence for those who doubted their existence.

The Andean people worship *huacas*, nature deities whose attributes and characteristics are similar to those of the Japanese *kami*. A *huaca* is an object or phenomenon with spiritual power or presence, in which the sacred is manifest, or the memory of some momentous event is imprinted.

On The Island of the Sun in the midst of Lake Titicaca, high in the Peruvian Andes, is a great stone

8 metres (25 feet) high and 58 metres (190 feet) long. In the local Aymara language it's called *Titi* ('wild cat') *kaka* ('rock'). This ancient *huaca* was once protected by a massive wall. Worshippers passed through three gates, one after another, confessing their sins and transgressions before entering the sacred precinct. The surrounding temples had elaborate carved doorways oriented towards the distant snow-capped peaks of Mount Sorata. Thus, as in Tibet, mountain and lake symbolised the creative duality, the father and mother of all things.

A Spanish eyewitness describes how images of the golden sun father Inti, his silver consort the moon mother Mama Quilla and a 'man of silver' representing the Thunder God were taken on reed boats from a shrine on the shore of Titicaca to a plaza in front of the Great Rock on the Island of the Sun. Elaborate jewellery, brightly coloured feather shields and ornate flower arrangements adorned and surrounded the statues before which the Inca priests and nobles prostrated themselves. At the conclusion of the ceremony the participants blew kisses to the gods and the massive *huaca* behind them.

The ritual may have its origins in an event that took place on the other side of the world in Sumatra 75,000 years ago when the greatest volcanic explosion in history filled the atmosphere with ash and debris, plunging the earth into the darkness of the last Ice Age. Imagine the fear and terror that must have followed the disappearance of the sun. Elders and shamans would have interceded with the god who had turned his back on them; but there was no answer, no light in the silent darkness. Then finally one day the sun appeared once more and life returned to normal.

The Collao people who live on the shores of Lake Titicaca have a story about this. Long ago, they say, there was a time when the sun vanished and great suffering followed. Crops failed and many died. Every day the people prayed to the sun god begging for the light of forgiveness.

Their prayers were answered when the sun rose up out of the island in the lake to warm the world again. There was a great celebration. Then from the southern part of the lake came a large white man with a silver beard who made mountains out of valleys and flat plains out of great heights. Like Moses, he struck rocks with his magic staff and springs of sweet water flowed from them. This being was the Supreme Creator, the Father of the Sun. They called him Ticciviracocha. His home was Lake Titicaca, the bottomless container of the mother fluid from which all forms came forth.

Lake Toba, in northern Sumatra, is the water-filled excavation created by the explosion of energy that led to the vanishing of the sun in Peru. It is the largest lake in southeast Asia, and one of the deepest (500 metres/1666 feet) in the world. Paddling a dugout canoe out from the shore, I was conscious of the dark abyss below the clear surface of the water sparkling in the early morning light.

Samosir Island in the middle of Lake Toba is the original home of the Toba Batak, a proud, flamboyant and warlike tribe, who trace their lineage back to a time when any stranger who looked upon them was killed and eaten. Cannibalism stopped in 1906 and now the island with its high-peaked traditional wooden houses is a thriving tourist destination.

In one of these houses built out over the lake I experienced the life of a lake dweller for a week or two. It was a life I didn't want to leave. I remembered Henry Thoreau's description of Walden Pond as 'a mirror no stone can crack, whose quicksilver will never wear off, whose gilding nature continuously repairs . . . a mirror in which all impurity presented to it sinks, swept and dusted by the sun's hazy brush'. Surrounded by the reflections of sky and mountains I spent hours watching the patterns and movements of birds and clouds until my mind drifted off with them across the mirror of the lake.

Some Muslim mystics see the created world as a mirror whose face may be compared to heaven and whose back is analogous to the earth. Divine wisdom is reflected in this mirror, wrote the Sufi poet Jalal al Din Rumi (1207–1273), and it is possible, he maintains, for the sincere seeker after truth to absorb wisdom directly from the mirror, without recourse to masters or sacred texts.

Days passed as I meditated on the mirror. I decided to stay another week so that I could enjoy the spectacle of the full moon 'washing its soul' in the waters of Lake Toba. Watching the golden moon slowly rise to cast its reflected image into a perfectly still lake is a deeply profound spiritual experience, one that unites us with the eternal mystery that has no name.

Gaining enlightenment is like the moon reflected in water, say the wise men of Zen. The moon does not get wet nor is the water disturbed.

Lakes invite us to explore and to meditate on their depths, until we find their harmony reflected in the lake of our own imagination.

# The Stream of Enlightenment

There shone in his face the serenity of knowledge, of one who is no longer confronted with the conflict of desires, who has found salvation, who is in harmony with the stream of events, full of sympathy and compassion, surrendering himself to the stream, belonging to the unity of all things.

Herman Hesse
*Siddhartha*

'There is a secret sweetness in the stream,' whispers Alfred Lord Tennyson. Streams invite us to explore this 'secret sweetness', their song draws us closer, all the better to hear. A famous Zen teaching story goes like this:

> 'Will you show me the way to Zen?' asked the monk.
> 'Can you hear the murmur of the mountain stream?' inquired the master.
> 'I do,' replied the monk.
> 'That is the Entrance.'

The murmur of the mountain stream is not the sound of human speech, but that of music. Music has its origins in nature, in the songs of birds, the rush of wind, the howling of wolves, the dripping of rain, the rhythmic beat of waves and the rolling of thunder. If life is motion then sound is its audible manifestation. All sound, natural or artificial, is vibration and all of creation vibrates and resonates.

At its peak of perfection, music is a harmonious composition of sounds that evokes emotions, images, feelings and even visions. We do not know how or why it does this. There is no scientific explanation for the effect of music on the human psyche, for its power to generate laughter, ecstasy, tears or reverence. If we can learn to listen to birdsong or a running stream with the same intensity with which we listen to music, we can immerse ourselves in unique harmonies that communicate directly to the ear and the spirit— to our outer and inner being.

A stream is a meeting place. If we are serious about wanting to listen to nature in general, and water in particular, then it is helpful to practise non-discrimination, to abandon judgement, and not distinguish critically between things or sounds, but to see them instead as a symphony, a divine composition created just for that moment, never to be repeated. Frogs, birds, cicadas, people even, are only there at that precise moment because the water has drawn them there.

Contemplative listening relies on intention. If our intention is to surrender our preconceptions in order to be in the presence of the Divine then, if we are fortunate, we may hear the Voice of the Supreme Intelligence. The Vedas call this voice, *Nada Brahma*, the celestial sound that animates the universe. 'The Creation speaks a universal language, independently of human speech or human language,' Tom Paine reminded an audience in one of his fiery speeches on the subject of American independence.

Sometimes I hear it too, echoing through the trees, rising up from the water, the Voice. And then suddenly it's gone and I'm left wondering . . .

For ten years I've listened intently to a pristine stream that flows out of a mountain half an hour's walk from my house. Every day I go to drink, bathe, sit and listen, open to learning whatever the water wants to teach.

I know this stream intimately from source to sea. Together we've been through times of scarcity and abundance, joy and sadness, drought and flood, summer and winter, spring and autumn. It's spring as I write, and bright yellow native shrubs shade the forest path, shedding blossoms in a carpet underfoot. The surface of the pool where I bathe shimmers with their golden petals and the grove that encloses it is perfumed with the scent of wildflowers.

Every day I make the same journey through the bush, climbing over rocks and fallen trees, following the stream back up past the high waterfall to the bathing pool. In my right hand I carry a black bamboo staff, a gift from the ocean, delivered to the beach by a high tide years ago. My backpack holds empty water bottles, to be filled with the day's drinking water, and a thin Japanese linen towel.

Walking is part of my ritual of preparing for bathing by letting go of the things of the world. North American Indians call it 'walking in a sacred manner'. 'If we can transform our walking path into a field for meditation, our feet will take every step in full awareness,' writes the Vietnamese sage, Thich Nhat Hanh. 'Our breathing will be in harmony with our steps and our mind will naturally be at ease. Every step we take will reinforce our peace and joy and cause a stream of calm energy to flow through us. Then we can say 'with every step a gentle wind blows'.

Sometimes there is a surprise waiting on the path.

Once I met a koala. Koalas are timid creatures and I had never before seen one in the wild. Remembering the advice of Konrad Lorenz, I crouched down as low as possible to diminish any perceived threat, and slowly moved closer to the animal who was walking unsteadily in the opposite direction. When we were about a metre apart, the bear sat down, turned around and looked at me with some curiosity. I returned his gaze. We were both mildly intoxicated, he from eucalyptus leaves, me from a couple of psilocybin mushrooms I'd found growing beside a stand of wild orchids.

We looked deeply into each other's eyes. His were large and brown and deep. They seemed to absorb my attention, drawing it into their warmth and my consciousness along with it. In that channel of communication, the voice of the koala said in a low tone, 'You may think that I am as small as I seem, but in reality I am very big', and, as I watched, his form seemed to expand, growing larger and larger until it towered above me kneeling before it, looking up. A brief moment of fear and astonishment and then the illusion was gone, and there was the creature still looking fixedly into my eyes. As I watched he turned and walked slowly to a nearby tree, climbing until I could no longer see him.

Whatever had passed between us gave me the feeling of being accepted by the forest, of being trusted. When you come to the same place at the same stream every day, eventually you become part of an extended family of birds, animals, insects and reptiles who live nearby and come every day too. You may feel as if you're alone but many eyes are watching. When creatures feel they can trust you they may choose to reveal themselves.

One day, a large lace monitor lizard appeared tiptoeing delicately down to where I stood naked, drying myself in the sun. This was unusual. Monitor lizards tend to avoid humans. Slowly, deliberately, taking no notice of me, he examined every item of clothing spread out on the rock, licking each with his darting forked tongue. Then he looked up at me, as if in some sort of acknowledgement, made his way across the stream, climbed the opposite bank and disappeared into the bush.

If we accept the idea that Divinity manifests itself in all things, meanings and significances appear that were previously invisible to us. For me, the action of the monitor was a blessing, to someone else it may just have been a cheeky lizard. On my daily pilgrimages I had similar encounters with a rock python, an old death adder, a wedgetail eagle, countless lyrebirds and a pair of friendly black cockatoos with crimson symbols on their inner wing feathers.

When I reach my destination, there's a place where I like to sit surrounded by the sound of water moving, falling, bubbling; some tones are treble, others bass. Below me in a glass-transparent pool, vibrations from the cascades' fall create rippling concentric patterns on the surface.

Projected onto the rocks and trees around the bank, the sunlit reflection of the circular waves produces a shimmering crystal lightshow, a symphony of movement, sound and energy, a fleeting glimpse of timeless rhythms of the universe.

I think of this as my sacred space.

Not 'mine' in the sense of ownership, but mine because it's where I feel welcomed and loved completely, unconditionally. Here my heart has learned to open itself to whatever gifts the water sends. I feel that this tranquil space has chosen me, rather than the other way round. 'Heaven and earth determine the places,' the *I Ching* tells us. 'The holy sages fulfil the possibilities of the places. Through the thoughts of men and the thoughts of spirits, the people are enabled to participate in the possibilities.'

Here I, too, have been 'enabled to participate in the possibilities'.

If you fix your attention on a point, either in a stream or at its edge, and remain focused, you will discover that flowing water has a pulse not unlike that of the human circulatory system, but slower. This water is alive—it is a living entity—literally a stream of consciousness. Contemplation of moving water allows us to align our consciousness with that of the stream and thereby absorb something of its energy. This is how we connect with the wisdom of water. The gateway to enlightenment. 'As you penetrate the flowing and not-flowing of water, the ultimate character of all things is instantly realised,' a Buddhist sutra asserts.

How do we approach this mystery? How can this change in consciousness be effected?

'The water knows everything,' Abraham Kavaii, a Hawaiian *Kahuna* told me once. I didn't believe him at the time, but now I think he was right. 'You can sit beside running water with your problems or questions, and if you ask in the right way the answers will come to you,' said Abraham. 'You may think it is your conscious mind that has come up with the solution, but it is the water in your brain that is remembering.

If you let go of ego thought and allow the spirit to do its work unimpeded the answer will come. It comes from the water. That's why we call it a 'solution'.

The German 'Water Wizard', Viktor Schauberger, was one who utilised this source of wisdom. Although Schauberger only had a rudimentary education, he was able to enunciate and demonstrate the highly technical principles of rocket and jet propulsion in universal use today. He created the first functioning rotary engines and circular flying machines. His scientific understanding came, he said, not from books or academic study, but from water:

> Even in my earliest youth my fondest desire was to understand nature and through such understanding to come closer to truth; a truth I was unable to discover either at school or in church. In this quest I was thus drawn, time and time again, into the forest. I could sit for hours on end and watch the water flowing by without ever becoming tired or bored. At the time I was still unaware that in water lay hidden the greatest secret. Nor did I know that water was the carrier of life or the *ur-*source of what we call consciousness. Without any preconceptions, I simply let my gaze fall on the water as it flowed past. Only years later

did I come to realise that running water attracts our consciousness like a magnet and draws a small part of it along in its wake. It is a force that can act so powerfully that one temporarily loses consciousness and involuntarily falls asleep.

Gradually I began to play a game with water's secret powers; surrendering my free consciousness and allowing the water to take possession of it for a while. Little by little this game turned into a profoundly earnest venture because I realised that one could detach one's own consciousness from the body and attach it to that of the water. When my own consciousness eventually returned, the water's most deeply concealed psyche often revealed the most extraordinary things to me. As a result of this investigation a researcher was born who could dispatch his consciousness on a voyage of discovery.

In the language of the Cogui who live in the remote mountains of Columbia, the word for 'creation' is 'water thinking'. Water thinking. Think about that for a minute—with your brain which is 9 per cent water! Could the Cogui be right? What if water is the 'mysterious' creative energy that flows through everything, the common bond we share with all animate and inanimate things? Think about Lao-Tzu's description of the Tao.

> The great Tao flows everywhere,
> To the left and to the right,
> All things depend on it to exist,
> And it does not abandon them.
> To its accomplishments it lays no claim.
> It loves and nourishes all things,
> But does not lord it over them.

Substitute the word 'water' for 'great Tao', and read it again. Could water indeed be the great Tao? And consider this from the *Huai Nan Tzu*: 'The Tao of Heaven operates mysteriously and secretly; it has no fixed shape; it follows no definite rules; it is so great that you can never come to the end of it; it is so deep that you can never fathom it.' All these qualities can be applied to water in its various manifestations. Lao Tzu calls the Tao, the Mysterious Feminine, the Cosmic Womb from which poured the waters that heralded the birth of the ten thousand things.

Here's another thought. In Hindu cosmology the *Akasha* is used to signify the omnipresent, all-penetrating existence. Everything that has form evolves out of the *Akasha*, the first of the five elements, the others being air, fire, earth and water.

The *Akasha* is the medium that *becomes* all things and to which all things return. Some esoteric philosophers have postulated the linked concept of a universal memory, the *Akasha Chronica*, the record of everything that has been thought or felt or done since the beginning of time. Many believe that water is the medium by which it can be accessed.

Is this the source of the wisdom that communicated itself to Schauberger in the flowing stream?

Other German philosophers, among them Goethe, Herman Hesse, Rudolf Steiner and Thomas Mann, have written of similar experiences. Mann described his in *A Man and His Dog* (1925):

> . . . I gladly profess that the contemplation of water in all kinds of manifestations and forms signifies by far the most immediate and insistent way of enjoying nature. Certainly the real state of contemplation, true oblivion, the real dissolution of one's own limited existence into the universal, is granted to me only in this experience.

Another who derived valuable insights from observing flowing streams is Edward de Bono. With more than forty books on the subject to his credit, Dr Edward de Bono is regarded by many as an authority on creative thinking. In 1993, de Bono turned his attention to water. In his book, *Water Logic*, he examines in some detail the 'flow behaviour' of creative thinking processes. De Bono outlines two different approaches to problem solving: flowing 'water logic', which focuses on constructive movement towards a goal or solution, as opposed to the rigid immovable 'rock logic' of science, economics, mathematics and the 'status quo'.

'Rock is hard, unchanging and unyielding,' he says, 'water is soft and yielding. A rock cannot change its shape to adapt to its surroundings whereas shapeless water adjusts itself to the container. Add one rock to another and you get two rocks. Add one water to another water and it merges to become one.'

Since our minds are in constant flow, de Bono argues, and thought is neither solid nor permanent, rock logic cannot usefully solve conceptual problems. Water logic, on the other hand, is the logic of the inner world of perception. One of the most compelling arguments in favour of water logic is, of course, the example of a rock in a stream. Not only does the stream flow around the immovable obstacle, it eventually erodes it away. There is the oft-quoted example offered by Lao Tzu in the *Tao Te Ching*:

> Nothing in the world is more flexible and
>     yielding than water,

Yet when it attacks the firm and the strong
   none can withstand it . . .
So the flexible overcomes the adamant, the
   yielding overcomes the forceful . . .

I am constantly reminded of this by the stream I visit. For millions of years, water has imprinted the pattern of its creative mind on the sandstone bed, carving its circular signature as clearly and precisely as any sculptor, relentlessly smoothing and polishing any rough edges into harmonious symmetry. This eternal process of dissolution that transforms sandstone back into sand continues even as I watch the water effort-lessly dancing silver in the sun.

There's an old Zen aphorism that says 'If you want to understand the teaching of water, then drink'. But that was long ago, before the age of pollution. Drinking from streams whose source is not known to you can be risky. Such water is better boiled. If you can satisfy yourself that the water is not contaminated, then drink slowly, one sip at a time, and savour the taste of the water's history and its origins.

To the disinterested and the uninitiated all water tastes the same. But every wild stream has its own character and subtle undertones, some pleasant, some powerful, others less so. The discernment of the tea masters of Sung Dynasty China in matters of water and taste was legendary.

*The Classic of Tea* by Lu Yu (764 AD), is one of the most informative and authoritive books on this subject. In a long section on water, Lu Yu writes that water from slow-flowing streams, stone-lined pools or milk-pure springs is the best mountain water. 'Never take tea made from water that falls rapidly in cascades, gushes from springs, rushing in a torrent that eddies and surges as if nature were rinsing its mouth.' Lu Yu even maintains that water from various locations in the same stream has differing qualities. One particular tea, Yang Hsien, prescribed as a remedy for pulmonary disease, was only supposed to be effective if made with water from the second of three rapids at Nanling on the Yangtse River.

A nobleman who had engaged Lu Yu to make Yang Hsien tea for him, sent a trusted servant especially to Nanling, instructing him to fill his jar at the middle rapid. On his return, Lu Yu scooped up some of the water and sipped it carefully. 'This is from the Yangtze but it's not from Nanling,' he pronounced. 'This tastes like water drawn from nearer the bank.' The servant protested that it was indeed from the rapid at the centre of the river. Lu Yu said nothing. Sending for another jar, he transferred water into it until only half remained. Then he tasted again, and smiled.

'From here on down is the water of Nanling. Is that not so?'

The astonished servant replied: 'I must confess that I did take the water from Nanling but, as I approached the bank, the boat began to rock and half the water spilt. So I refilled the jar near the bank as you have said. Truly your powers of discrimination are like a God's!' While we mortals may not possess such extraordinary powers of discrimination, it is helpful to develop one's capacity to taste and distinguish one water from another.

Traditional Tibetan medicine texts enumerate the desirable qualities of pure water in the following description of The Spring of Seven Hundred Thousand Powers:

> This is the water possessing the eight good qualities:
> Lightness, clearness, coolness, softness,
> Purity, sweetness, stomach-soothingness, cure for all diseases;

In the absence of such a stream even tap water—if treated with reverence—can quench both bodily and spiritual thirst if drunk in a sacred manner. To drink with awareness from the endless stream of consciousness you do not necessarily need to travel to some far-off destination, but if you do make the journey you can connect with another aspect of wild water.

The word *baptism* comes from the Greek '*baptein*' meaning to plunge, to immerse, to wash. Ritual immersion, bathing in a sacred manner to cleanse and purify the spirit, dates back to a time when the divinity of water was unquestioned. Baptism invoked the blessing and protection of the spirit of the terrestrial waters for those who had recently emerged from the waters of the womb.

Its practice is ancient and universal. The Egyptian *Book of Going Forth by Day* prescribes instructions for the baptism of newborns in Nile water to wash away impurities acquired in the womb. The Aztecs had a ceremony which began with a prayer to Chalchiutlicue, the Jade Goddess of Running Water. 'Behold him between thy hands,' intoned the priest as he bathed the infant; 'Wash him and deliver him from impurities . . . Cleanse him of the contamination he has received from his parents; let the water wash away the soil and the stain and let him be freed from all taint.'

Baptism has other significances for adults. In the first centuries of the Christian era, baptism in streams was the beginning of a process of initiation into the mysteries of Christianity, in which the spiritual eyes of the novice were symbolically opened to the light of God that shines in all creation. Those who received this knowledge were spoken of as 'the enlightened ones'. 'Be baptised with the flowing water from the world of light,' says the *Right Ginza* of the Mandaeans, Middle Eastern Christians who clothe themselves in white to better imitate 'the mystery of the flowing water'. 'Baptised, we are enlightened,' wrote Clement of Alexandria in the third century; 'Enlightened we are adopted; adopted we are made perfect; perfect, we become immortal.'

Enlightenment.

This is the aspect of baptism that seizes my imagination, the bath of renewal and regeneration. 'Jump into the river with your clothes on', urges the *Magic Papyrus* of the Egyptians. 'After immersing yourself, come out, change your clothes and depart without looking back.' This rite was intended to awaken the spirit of the initiate so that he (or she) could hear the oracular voice of the divine and receive its teaching.

Personally, I prefer to leave my clothes on the bank and bathe naked whenever circumstances permit, just as our ancestors did. Many North American Indian warriors immersed themselves daily in cold running water, even if there was ice floating in it. Aside from any spiritual regeneration so obtained this practice improves blood circulation, invigorates the body and strengthens the immune system.

According to Professor Vijay Kakkar of London's Thrombosis Research Institute, regular immersion in cold water boosts production of testosterone, the hormone that regulates sexual potency in men, and oestrogen in women. Increasing female oestrogen levels improves fertility, so stories about infertile women bathing in sacred ponds and streams in order to become pregnant could have a 'scientific' basis. Sometimes it takes us hundreds of years to verify scientifically what indigenous people know intuitively.

Sacred bathing means moving consciously into the water (rather than diving or plunging), retaining an awareness that we are participating in an ancient ritual of power. Immersed, the body becomes weightless, and without weight to manoeuvre, mind becomes lighter. Supported, we float without effort, our movements those of the aquatic creatures that we once were in the womb so long ago. It is a return, a remembering. Rocked in the arms of our mother, we can let go of volition and merge our consciousness with hers.

This is where I come to pray, offering myself up to the will of the water, asking her to teach me what I most need to know, to guide my steps that day. Underwater, I open my eyes to the shifting patterns of sunlight penetrating its iridescent depths. Here is another world inhabited by water's creations, our natural brothers and sisters.

One day, while standing in the pool lost in contemplation, I felt a tug on the nail of my big toe where a persistent fungal infection was proving difficult to dislodge. Looking down I saw a small yabbie, a miniature freshwater crayfish, cleaning beneath my nail with its tiny claws, removing impurities in a practical sense. These tiny crustaceans are hunted relentlessly by children and adults for their aquariums or perhaps for some sort of connection with the last vestiges of wildness. So yabbies, or at least those that survive, have learned to hide under rocks or in crevices until predatory humans have departed. Yet here was this tiny creature approaching me without fear, with love.

I was deeply moved.

Later that year I saw a mother yabbie, perhaps the same one, walking slowly on the sandy bottom not far from me with her brood of babies nestled beneath the protection of her tail. Was she proudly showing them to me as an intimate member of her extended family?

I like to think so.

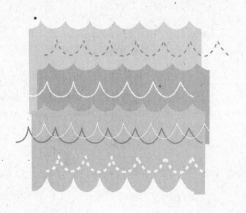

# The Ocean of Awareness

I am the boundless ocean
This way and that,
The wind blowing where it will
Drives the ship of the world,
But I am not shaken.
I am the unbounded deep
In whom the waves of all the worlds
Naturally rise and fall,
But I do not rise or fall.
I am the infinite deep
In whom all of the worlds
Appear to rise.
Beyond all form,
Forever still
Even so am I.

*The Ashtavakra Gita,* 400 BC

Stanislaw Lem's science fiction novel *Solaris* describes a space station on a distant planet where there's an ocean which thinks and plans and creates illusions that seem real in order to get to know the minds and emotions of humans. What if our ocean was a living thinking entity like the one on Solaris? How do we know that it isn't?

Creation stories the world over point to the great unbounded deep as the origin, the source of all life. Before time, the *Rig Veda* tells us:

> Neither Non-Being nor Being existed then.
> Neither air nor the firmament above existed.
> What was moving with such force? Where?
>    Under whose care?
> Was it the deep and fathomless water?

Even today we know very little about the sea around us, even though it covers three-quarters of the planet. A vast proportion of the world's oceans, 97 per cent in all, are more than 200 metres (665 feet) deep. They remain largely unknown and unexplored. As an eminent marine biologist recently observed, 'There are more footsteps on the moon than there are on the bed of the sea'.

Our marine ancestors crawled from this same sea millions of years ago. The salinity of our blood is similar to that of seawater. We begin our life as fish with foetal gills and a few of us retain them into adult-hood. I once had the pleasure of meeting a woman with gills at a party in Sydney. Knowing my obsession with water and (at that time) mermaids, my hostess invited her to meet me. Her name was Jenny. She worked for the Sydney Water Board.

Jenny was quite proud of her gills. She has been the subject of countless examinations, several scans and numerous scientific papers.

'Could I touch them?' I asked.

'Be my guest,' she said, lifting her chin and offering her throat for my inspection.

As gills go Jenny's were disappointing. They were vestigial and similar to the 'Adam's Apple' of a male. She couldn't breathe underwater, she said laughing as I gently probed the strange growth. There in the middle of a noisy party I felt as if I was touching an ancient mystery.

Were we once human fish, brothers and sisters to the dolphins, seals and dugongs who chose to remain in the security of the sea? Hints of aquatic adaptation in humans include our erect posture, our slightly webbed hands and feet, our ability to dive and swim, and the subcutaneous layer of fat which, some say, replaced the fur that once covered our bodies.

In her controversial work on evolution, *The Aquatic Ape*, Elaine Morgan argues that humans are descended from ape-like creatures who were forced into the sea aeons ago in order to survive. And it was in the sea, during the million years that our ancestors dwelt there, that they moved through the evolutionary processes and changes which distinguish humans from other animals. It was there, too, that they acquired enough physical dexterity and ego to impose their will on the rest of the natural world.

This could explain the comparatively recent discovery that babies can swim, not merely before they can walk, but before they can crawl. Charles Ramsay, a swimming instructor who works with infants observed, 'During the first year of their lives they have an inborn reflex which stops them breathing during short spells under the surface. As a result no water can get into their lungs. They have remarkable breath control, which they lose when they are over a year old. Nobody can explain why. But at this age they will not cough or panic under water. They also have a natural buoyancy because of their fatty tissue, which they lose when they start to crawl or walk. But at the age we get them, they have no fear of water. It is virtually impossible for them to come to any harm even when they are placed face down on the surface of the pool'.

Obstetrician Michel Odent and Jessica Johnson documented water birth and the subsequent activities of aquatic infants in their lavishly illustrated book *We are all Water Babies*. Johnson's underwater photography is a creative celebration of babies swimming back in time, back to that first momentous immersion.

Travelling in Africa in 1934, British anthropologist, Geoffrey Gorer went to Senegal because he had heard that some members of the Wolof tribe could breathe underwater. He was told that this hereditary gift was confined to a few families, and needed training to be developed. Gorer asked for a demonstration and a diver volunteered. 'I chose the place where he was to dive,' Gorer recorded, 'where the water was particularly limpid and asked him to stop at the bottom for twenty minutes. He stopped there for three quarters of an hour. I had him continuously in view and he had no apparatus of any kind; occasionally he would send up an air bubble to the surface. At the end of the period he came up to ask if he had stayed down long enough. To all my inquiries as to how he did it he replied that "he breathed like a fish" which didn't advance matters much.'

Nicholas Persée was a famous Sicilian diver in the twelfth century who could remain under water for long periods of time—45 minutes, according to one account. He had webbed feet and hands (not uncommon even today), lived mainly on raw fish and swam among the Lipuri Islands, where he made a living diving for pearls and delivering letters in a waterproof bag.

Nicholas was often accompanied in his travels by dolphins. Humans and dolphins have a long history of dynamic interaction. The statue of the sea goddess Atargatis of Khirbet Tannur in ancient Palestine was that of a dolphin-tailed deity, her headdress crowned by two leaping dolphins. At her temples in pre-Hellenic Crete dolphins were accorded divine status.

Along the Vietnamese coast I saw elaborately deco-rated dolphin temples, where the dead 'Mandarins of the Sea' are buried in special graveyards with full ceremonial honours. This practice was formalised by a Vietnamese Emperor in the eighteenth century as a token of his gratitude to a pod of dolphins who saved some sailors from drowning during a war with China. Helpless in the water after their ship was sunk by the Chinese, the sailors were kept afloat by dolphins. The resulting morale boost to the Vietnamese Navy from this intervention enabled them to win the strategic battle.

In the Pacific islands, dolphins are messengers of the Gods, ancestral spirits who guide canoes, rescue drowning humans and sometimes help with the fishing. The Wanungamulangwa people of Groote Eylandt on the north coast of Australia trace their ancestry back to the Injebena, bottlenose dolphins who live in the deep water offshore. The young learn from their elders how to communicate with dolphins and how to fish co-operatively with them. 'I used to go out fishing with my uncle who had studied dolphins for many years,' said one. 'When he called them, three dolphins would appear at the sides of the boat and one at the back. They would then make a field of sound that would drive a whole mob of fish into shore.'

The word 'dolphin' is derived from the Greek *Delphys*, meaning womb; Delphi was 'the womb of the world' where Apollo, the God of Light, appeared in the form of a dolphin. There are many old Greek stories about dolphins; one connects their origin with Dionysus, the Deity of Drunken Ecstasy.

Dionysus had hired a boat to take him from the Island of Ikaria to the Island of Naxos. The sailors were a crew of pirates who, not realising that their rich passenger was a God in disguise, planned to kidnap and rob him then sell him into slavery. Sailing past Naxos the ship headed towards Egypt. Dionysus responded by transforming the oars into serpents and filling the ship with ivy while an orchestra of invisible flutes played eerie music. Wreathed in vines the ship lost its way. One by one the sailors went insane, leaping overboard into the sea where they became dolphins whose eternal task was to assist humans in difficulties.

There was plenty for them to do.

Around 600 BC, according to the historian Herodotus, devotees at the Temple of the Goddess on the Greek island of Lesbos were regularly enchanted by the music of Arion, a harpist of extraordinary talent. When he sang of heroes his voice assumed a depth and power which evoked the Gods, when he sang of the sweetness of love it was said that the strings of his harp whispered to the hearts of all who listened.

Arion became renowned throughout Greece. At the court of King Periander in Corinth he created the dithyramb, a new form of song which accompanied the royal dancers. Famous, wealthy and laden with gifts and prizes accumulated in his travels, Arion hired a ship to take him home.

The envious sailors decided to throw Arion overboard and keep his money. Like Dionysus, Arion guessed their intentions. He offered them everything if they would spare his life, but they feared he would report them to the King. Since death seemed unavoidable Arion decided to meet it singing. Putting on his robes, he stood in the stern of the boat and sang for his captors. When the last notes were played Arion turned and plunged over the side into the sea. But, says Plutarch:

> Before his body was entirely submerged, dolphins swam beneath him, and he was

borne upward, full of doubt and uncertainty and confusion at first. But when he began to feel at ease . . . the many dolphins gathering around him in a friendly way . . . there came into his thoughts, as he said, not so much a feeling of fear in the face of death, or a desire to live, as a proud longing to be saved that he might be shown to be a man loved by the gods and that he might gain a sure opinion regarding them.

Brought safely to shore, Arion returned to Corinth. The King captured and executed the pirates, returning all that they had stolen. In the Temple of the Sea Goddess, Arion left an offering of thanks—a small bronze figure of a man riding a dolphin.

River dolphins have a reputation for saving humans in South America. The Amazon dolphin, the *boto*, has rescued people from capsized boats, protecting them from attack by piranha fish. The boto is revered by Amazon fishermen who release any caught in their nets, and beg their pardon.

Strange stories and superstitions surround the boto. Zoologist Janusz Talalaj tells of 'a peculiar belief among these Indians that the dolphin is very fond of young girls and during carnivals disguises himself as a man. If an unmarried girl becomes pregnant the Indians believe it to be the result of a dolphin's love and the girl is not disgraced in the community.' After dark, male and female botos rise up from their underwater city, turn into white people with different coloured eyes, four-fingered hands and blowholes hidden under their sombreros and come ashore to seduce unsuspecting partners and coax them back into the river.

Most animals indulge in sexual activity for the purpose of reproduction. In this they differ from higher primates and cetaceans like dolphins and whales, who engage in sex for pleasure or as social interaction. However, the dolphin is the only one known to approach humans to initiate sexual play.

One such encounter occurred in 1972 off the northwest coast of Spain near the fishing village of La Corogna, where a female bottlenose dolphin called Nina struck up an intimate friendship with Luis Salleres, a local clam diver. At first people in the town refused to believe Salleres' story. When they found that he was telling the truth, Nina became a Spanish national heroine, attracting flocks of tourists. She mixed freely with bathers on the beach permitting them to pat her and even to ride on her back.

In *Dolphins*, Jacques Cousteau describes how Renoir, one of his diving team, spent a week filming and scuba diving with Nina. Initially she rubbed the whole length of her body against Renoir. When he stroked her, she rolled over on her back in 'a position characteristic of females in heat'. Renoir extended his hand and Nina rubbed her clitoris against it.

'We played together for thirty or forty-five minutes,' Renoir recalls. 'There always came a time when Nina began leaping into the air, then she would fall back and return to me, wildly eager for more fun and games. It was an extraordinary situation, as though the barrier between man and animal no longer existed. There was some sort of strange understanding between us . . . Luis Salleres, the Spanish diver, had the same sort of feeling for Nina. In fact, he told me that his wife was jealous of the dolphin and sometimes made scenes over her.'

The seal is another marine creature which has close ties with humans. Many families in fishing communities in Iceland and the Gaelic world of Scotland, Ireland and the Hebrides, claim descent from seals. The progeny of the union of seals and humans possess the gifts of prophecy and clairvoyance, and because of their aquatic heritage, they cannot drown. There are rumours that seals are reincarnated sinners, fallen angels or descendants of Pharaoh's ill-fated army who drowned by the flooding of the Red Sea. Seals are often spoken of as the Sea People.

The killing of a seal is no light matter. Many believe that it brings bad fortune. 'There is no luck' said an Irish fisherman, 'in the presence of a seal that is dead'. Seal hunting is violent, cruel work. 'Ouch boys! Spare your old grandfather Darby O'Dowd', one great seal is said to have cried just as it was about to be clubbed to death by some Irish sealers.

An old story from John O'Groat's in northeastern Scotland tells of a professional sealer, Angus MacRitchie, who was changed into a seal. One evening, a stranger on horseback galloped into the yard of MacRitchie's stone cottage. Dismounting, the black-cloaked figure introduced himself as the agent of a wealthy hatter who wished to place a large order for sealskins. His employer, who was staying at a nearby inn, was anxious to discuss the matter with MacRitchie that evening. The agent suggested that the sealer ride back with him immediately.

It was an offer too good to refuse. Kissing his wife goodnight, MacRitchie seated himself behind the rider and they galloped off into the darkness. After riding some distance they came to a great cliff high above the waves pounding on the seashore. To MacRitchie's astonishment the rider gripped him firmly and plunged his horse straight over the cliff into the sea. Descending into the depths, the two came at last to a door set in the rock face. When they entered, MacRitchie found himself in a cave crowded with seals. He looked down and found that, like the horseman, he too had been transformed into a seal.

The creatures greeted MacRitchie as an equal, but this was not a social occasion. His guide produced a great knife asking if he'd ever seen it before. As this was the weapon the hunter used regularly for killing and skinning seals, he could hardly deny ownership. The seal told him that one of the seals he had wounded was the speaker's own father, and according to the law of sympathetic magic, only the person who caused the wound could cure it. MacRitchie was led to the rear of the cavern where the suffering seal lay bleeding from a deep gash in his side. The hunter was ordered to lay his hand on the wound which, to his amazement, stopped bleeding and healed immediately.

Surrounded by the seal colony, MacRitchie was made to swear a solemn oath that never again would he kill a seal. He was then taken back to the shore where he was transformed back into a human, standing dry and alone on a seaweed-strewn beach in the light of the moon. Reaching into his pocket heavy with unaccustomed weight, MacRitchie found a leather purse containing a handful of antique gold coins. One, a Greek drachma from Phocia, bore on its surface the worn image of a seal.

The Phocians, one of the earliest tribes in Greece, acknowledged as the mother of their clan the nereid

Psmathe, the first seal maiden to appear in ancient records.

Psmathe was one of the fifty daughters of Nereus, the Old Man of the Sea. Like many nereids Psmathe was ardently pursued by several gods of whom the most persistent was Aeacus, son of Zeus. In order to avoid his unwelcome advances, Psmathe transformed herself into a seal but this did not make any difference. Still smitten, Aeacus forced the seal to submit to his passionate embrace and, as a consequence, a son Phocus was conceived. Phocus became the founder of the tribe which bears his name and is remembered in the Greek word for seal, *Phoce*.

It is probable that the Phocians, who revered seals as ancestors, were descended from a prehistoric clan who worshipped the seal as its totem. Sealskin robes were symbols of magic power in which the spirit of the shaman could enter the sea to consult the Deity. When he returned from his spirit journey and took off the sealskin, he became a man once more. Perhaps this dimly remembered mystery from times past, was the origin of the story of the seal woman who transforms magically into a human when she removes her skin and then back into a seal when she puts it on.

This is a modern version of a tale recorded by Jon Guomundsson the Learned in 1641. Even then it was old.

One evening, when the moon was bright, Olaf Magnusson, a lonely fisherman from Mrydal in Eastern Iceland, was walking beside the sea when he came to a large cave. There on the sand several seal-skins lay scattered in front of him. Inside he could see a circle of figures dancing naked in the firelight. Olaf had heard stories of such things when he was a child. Silently he reached down, picked up the skin nearest to him, folded it carefully and carried it back to his cottage. Wrapping it in a linen cloth, Olaf placed the package in the bottom of an old iron-bound sea chest which held his valuable possessions, and locked it securely.

Early next morning Olaf returned to the cave and found a naked young woman sitting on a rock weeping bitterly because she had lost her skin and could not return to the water. Her name, she said, was Gudrun. Olaf told her that he had taken the skin and he refused to return it. Instead he offered Gudrun a gift of clothes and invited her to live with him.

Reluctantly the seal maiden agreed. After a time the two grew quite fond of each other, married and had children like any other couple. Although she seemed happy, Gudrun did not mix with others in the village. Often she sat alone by the shore, staring out to sea. She was, however, an excellent mother and house-keeper and she kept the keys to all the rooms and storehouses in a ring on her belt. But there was one key Gudrun was never given because her husband kept it with him always. Many years passed and the house grew larger to accommodate their seven children. One Sunday as the family dressed for church Gudrun, pale and ill, decided to stay at home.

During the service Olaf felt in his pocket for the key. It was not there. He had left it in his work trousers. He ran as fast as he could to the house. The front door was wide open and so was the sea chest. He turned and ran towards the shore where he could see Gudrun standing on a rock among the waves, her face white—the rest of her body inside the sealskin. As he watched she dived into the sea.

Olaf was broken hearted at the loss of Gudrun and withdrew into himself. Soon, strange stories began to circulate in the village. It was said that whenever Olaf rowed out to fish, a seal swam around his boat with tears running from its eyes. Olaf became a very successful fisherman, and lucky too. Several valuable things were washed up in front of his cottage. And people noticed that when any of Olaf's seven children were walking on the seashore, a seal swam nearby in the sea, sometimes tossing them coloured fish and beautiful shells.

Shells are the ocean's artworks offered daily on the altar of the shore. The patterns on the surface of shells are the writing of water. The Sufi poet Shabistari likens the ocean to the Heart of the Great Mystery—its shores represent gnosis; shells are its written words. Within shells, pearls may sometimes be found. Pearls, he says, contain the knowledge of the heart, the key to the mysterious language of shells.

Every ancient alphabet contains letters derived from shell patterns. The letters 'e', 'c', 'g' for instance, are spiral shapes while 'n' and 'w' can be found in their original form ornamenting cone shells. For thousands of years shell patterns have been a source of inspiration, the infinite variety of their designs reflected in art, craft, weaving and pottery, from Peru to Scotland.

Among the most intriguing shells are the ammonites. Ammonites are fossils. The molluscs that originated them died out five hundred million years ago. Yet in their shells these tiny creatures articulated and demonstrated fundamental principles of architecture, engineering and mathematics that humans would later use to great effect. One of these was the practical application of the perfect logarithmic spiral we call the Golden Ratio.

I have one of these rare treasures, cut in half to reveal its exquisite symmetry. Holding it for the first time, I wondered how the ammonite, and its modern cousin, the chambered nautilus, came into existence. Each started with a tiny speck of accretion around which the mollusc built using precise mathematical formulae. Here's the unspoken question posed by its design. How did that original cell know what to do? Was there a model, a prototype, an original spiral expressing itself?

Then I realised that there, resting in my palm, was the signature symbol of water, set in stone. The spiral vortex expresses the endless movement of water, its curving waves, spinning currents, whirlpools, water-spouts, tornadoes and hurricanes.

The spiral also demonstrates the concept of eternity. It begins at a fixed point and continues to expand. It has a beginning but no end. From the largest galaxy to the microscopic structure of our DNA, the spiral vortex is the driving force, the ulti-mate expression of water's infinite creative energy.

Coming from a country where seaside real estate is highly prized (and highly priced) I was amazed at the comparatively deserted sea coast of northern Japan. I had assumed that everyone was as attracted to the shore as I was.

'Where are all the people?' I asked. 'Doesn't anyone want to live on the beach?'

My Japanese host's answer was brief and to the point. 'Tsunamis,' he said with a shrug.

I realised how fortunate I had been to grow up

beside the ocean without fear. I loved the long sandy beaches where I learned to bodysurf, to consign myself to the energy of a wave and let it carry me at high speed in to shore. I gathered oysters off the rocks and dug pippies out of the sands as the tide receded. For years I was a beachcomber, rising early so that mine would be the first footsteps of the day on the white coral sand.

Looking for rare cone and olive shells to sell to collectors I found other strange and wonderful things as well. There was a dead dugong whose precious ivory tusks I extracted; I made jewellery from exotic beans and seeds washed down from the jungle and carved driftwood timbers into forms that pleased me. I talked to seagulls, to the waves, to the wind.

Then years later the ocean spoke to me. It was a life-changing experience. For a long while I didn't talk about it because I thought that my friends would think that I'd lost my mind. Now I see the incident in the context of my life, I no longer care what anyone thinks.

This is what happened.

In 1989, I was deeply troubled by events in my life. Lonely, miserable and distressed, I retreated to Brunswick Heads, a fishing village on the north coast of New South Wales. Every day for months I swam and walked miles along the beach beside the rolling surf. The long walks soothed and exhausted me, bringing deep restful sleep, my appetite improved and the mists surrounding my heart began to lift. One evening I went to see *The Dead Poets' Society*. The movie reminded me of my years at boarding school. Driving home through the moonlit bush, one sentence resonated over and over in my mind: '*Carpe Diem*—seize the day', Robin Williams exhortation to his young pupils to make an adventure of life before it was too late.

I was thinking about this the next morning when the sea breeze riffled the pages of a magazine on the coffee table, exposing an aerial photograph of a chain of palm-fringed coral islands set in an azure sea. 'Come to Micronesia,' I read. Somehow it seemed like a personal invitation, an adventure, an offer.

'Carpe Diem,' I thought.

I rang magazine editors who commissioned stories then called the travel company who placed the ad. After a brief negotiation they agreed to send me to Micronesia for a month at their expense. My brief was to photograph and write about the culture of Micronesia in general, and the spectacular megalithic ruins in particular. As a writer on building and architecture, I was fascinated by ancient construction techniques, and I knew that off the island of Ponape there was a walled city in the sea made entirely of basalt crystals laid without mortar. The local people said that it had been built long ago by strangers, magicians who could make massive stones fly through the air. They called it Nan Madol, the Reef of Heaven.

Covering 70 hectares (11 square miles), Nan Madol consists of 92 man-made islands, laid out in squares linked by a network of canals, the whole protected by a massive breakwater several miles long. One astonished European visitor in the nineteenth century called it the Venice of the Pacific. The walls and foundations of each island are made of three metre-long (10 feet) hexagonal basalt crystal columns laid alternatively lengthwise and crosswise. Each column weighs about two tonnes.

It wasn't easy getting out to visit the Reef of Heaven. When I tried to charter a launch, none of the locals were enthusiastic. Most Ponapeans believe the place is watched over by the powerful spirits of those who built it. They didn't want to go there. But eventually I found myself in a hired boat with several companions making our way through the mangrove swamps to the black steaming buttresses of Nan Madol. We entered the labyrinth and coasted through still water and dragonflies; vines hung down from huge strangler figs whose roots twined into fantastic shapes. Here and there, lichen-encrusted stonework could be glimpsed through the silent dark-green shadows.

'The massive ruins of Ponape speak in their weird loneliness of some dead forgotten race,' Fredrick Moss had written in 1899.

Nothing had changed.

Turning a corner into a wide canal we were confronted by the fortress island of Nan Dowas, 'The Place of the Lofty Walls'. Within, lay the tombs of the Sandeleur Kings, protected by three sets of walls eight metres high and three metres thick (26 foot by 10 foot).

A light rain misted down as we entered through a wide stone gateway which opened directly onto the canal. A giant fig overhung one corner of the interior courtyard; misty steam rose from the hot black granite paving. The humidity was unbearably oppressive. In the middle of the court stood three basalt sarcophagi. Simple but imposing structures, they were virtually big stone boxes made from octagonal columns with roofs of the same material.

Back in 1899, F.W. Christian, an archaeologist, persuaded some Ponapeans to help clear the dense undergrowth in and around the crypts, but they didn't stay long. 'The eyes of the spirits are watching everything you do,' one frightened worker explained. 'They will not hurt you because you are a white man, but they will punish us. I cannot sleep at night; I am very much afraid, and I should like to go home.'

When the central tomb was cleared, Christian found 'a quart of rose-pink beads', made from seashells, 'very minute and delicate in design'. Some were round, others rectangular, 'identical' said Christian, 'to the *Wampum* or shell-bead money of the North American Indians, who use them for ornamenting pouches, moccasins and girdles'.

Each crypt is half buried in the moist earth so that, in order to enter, it's necessary to step down half a metre. Inside, the heat and humidity were stifling. The function of these monuments was to provide a space for the dead bodies of the nobility to decompose so that their remains could be fed to the Eel God, Nan Somohol, who lived in a pool on another island. In these conditions, decay would not take very long. My clothes were soaked with perspiration. It seeped from my pores and dripped down my forehead, running into my eyes as I adjusted a wide-angle lens to try to capture the interior.

The hand-held flash lit the scene for a brief second before it slipped from my hand and fell on the stone floor. The bottom burst open and the batteries spilled out. Kneeling down, I collected them one by one, knocking aside some moss as I did so. This exposed a tiny shell-like object wedged between the stones. I put it with the batteries in my jacket pocket and climbed back into the steaming courtyard where I spent another hour photographing the walls in detail, enchanted by their massive strangeness, and our guide's story of their creation.

According to tradition, Nan Madol was built by two brothers, Olo-chipa and Olo-chopa. By the magic spells of these men 'one by one the massive stone blocks flew through the air like birds, settling down into their appointed place'. The Ponapeans have great respect for the spiritual qualities of stone and particular stones are believed to possess great *mana*. In *Children of the Sun*, W.J. Perry talks of the cult worship of certain 'spirit' stones on Ponape. 'These stones,' he continues, 'are not only used in connection with offerings made to the gods, but also possess magical power and healing properties.'

The eerie sound of a blown conch shell called us back to the boat. 'You don't want to be out here after the sun sets,' said the skipper as we headed back to the other world.

Who were the sea worshippers of Nan Madol, I wondered, back in my thatched hotel bungalow, and why had they left after expending so much time and energy? The volume of stone they moved equals that of two of the largest Egyptian pyramids. It was hard to get my mind around it. When I emptied the contents of my pocket onto the table, among them was the flat piece of shell I'd found in the tomb. It was round, about the size of a one-cent piece, and white in colour. In the centre a hole had been drilled. It was a shell bead—perhaps an ancient one. I put it in the side pocket of my camera bag for luck, but when I looked for it days later, it had disappeared.

That night, dreams of the vast stone city lying empty and silent in the maze of moonlit canals haunted me. Shadowy figures moved in the foliage, the glittering waters teemed with unseen life, the invisible flesh-eating Eel God in his temple pool brooded over my sleep. When I woke the sheets were wet with perspiration. Night after night, the dream persisted.

Back in Agana, the capital of Guam, I set off in a hired car to photograph the interior of a famous cave in the Talafofo Hills. This cave contains prehistoric stone hieroglyphs thought to be from the Chamorro civilisation, the original inhabitants of Guam. I was told about it by an affable Guamanian I met in a late-night bar. When I asked whether he would come with me as a guide, my informant declined. 'Things happen up there—people say that the caves are guarded by the spirits of buried ancestors.' He gave me directions and a rough map drawn on the back of a beer coaster. 'Take care,' he said as I left.

At that time I didn't believe in spirits, gods or magic. It just seemed like a good story. The previous day I had gone down to explore the ocean in a large comfortable submarine equipped for tourists. We moved past sea caves where giant grouper sat unmoving like guardian gods; squids and cuttlefish propelled themselves above the waving seagrasses as the living world of a multi-coloured coral reef continued around us. It was a rare and precious vision.

'From the depths of the sea to the peaks of the mountains,' I thought, as I unpacked my cameras and tripod beside the rough dirt track that led up into the Talafofo Hills.

It soon became obvious that my map was useless. The hills were honeycombed with caves. I crouched down and ventured into one that looked promising. About five minutes in, my torch failed. A furry thing that felt like a large crab or spider ran across my sandalled foot. Startled, I banged my head on the roof of the cave. It seemed as if the spirits were trying to tell me something. I retreated back into the sunlight and continued slowly up to the summit where, I had been told, there was a special stone known as the Eye of the Needle.

It wasn't hard to see why they called this extraordinary monolith the Eye of the Needle. Its upper surface was pierced by an oval opening in the almond shape of a madorla. The hole was wide enough to accommodate me so I climbed up, sat comfortably down in the Eye, and looked out over the Pacific

Ocean stretched out below me. It was midday. The blue water sparkled with reflected sunlight which, as I watched, seemed to increase in intensity until it became difficult to look at directly.

Then I heard a voice. It seemed to be coming from the light, but I could hear it inside my head.

'I don't believe this,' I exclaimed out loud.

In spite of my disbelief a dialogue took place between us, the Voice and I. Overwhelmed by the feeling that the ocean was speaking, I asked questions and received answers. That's all I want to say. Then the experience was over and I was left sitting alone in the Eye of the Needle.

My mind was racing, trying to make sense of what had just happened. I thought of Joan of Arc and how she heard the voice of God calling to her. When she was examined by the English judges who sentenced her to death, Joan spoke with conviction of her dialogue with God. 'Surely,' said one exasperated judge, 'surely this all happened in your imagination?' 'But isn't that how God speaks to us, in our imagination?' the Maid of Orleans replied disingenuously.

I thought of Henry Wadsworth Longfellow's poem *The Sound of the Sea*, one of many I'd memorised during my schooldays.

> The sea awoke at midnight from its sleep,
> And round the pebbly beaches far and wide

I heard the first wave of the rising tide
Rush onward with uninterrupted sweep;
A voice out of the silence of the deep,
A sound mysteriously multiplied
As of a cataract from the mountain's side
Or roar of winds upon a wooded steep.
So comes to us at times, from the unknown
And inaccessible solitudes of being,
The rushing sea tides of the soul;
And inspirations that we deem our own,
Are some divine foreshadowing and
    foreseeing
Of things beyond our reason or control

'A voice out of the silence of the deep,' the line kept repeating itself to me.

I thought about the liquid imagination of my mind and the possibility that the vast mind of the ocean could reach out to the water within me.

Maybe that's what happened. All I know is that the person who climbed down from the Eye of the Needle was not the same person who had climbed up. Something definitely happened up there, something that dissolved my scepticism about the spirit world.

I had heard the Voice, of that I was certain.

Metaphorically and actually, I had seen the light.

I returned to Australia confident that my destiny was now in the hands of the Voice. As often as I could

I went to sit by the sea, convinced that I was under its care and protection. Water, in whatever form, became a source of fascination, obsession even. Six months later I wrote my first book on the subject. When I offered it to my mainstream publishers it was rejected.

'Too much of a polemic,' said one.

'Not enough interest,' said another.

I went ahead and published the book myself. Against all odds, during the first twelve months I had to reprint it five times. My bank account went from three digits to six, and more kept coming. Like most writers I had learned to live sparely. My material needs were few and easily satisfied. What should I do with this money I wondered?

I went to Lyndall, a close friend I trusted, a gifted clairvoyant.

She read the cards.

'This money has come from the water,' she told me, 'to facilitate your work. It is an auspicious sign that you are being supported. Do not spend it on frivolous things.'

I took her advice.

Immersing myself in a self-funded study of water, I was drawn to the maze of stories of the gods and goddesses of the sea. Regardless of expense, I accumulated an extensive library of books, on goddess lore, mythology, magic and marine biology. Some of the water's money I spent exploring the hot springs of New Zealand and Japan, visiting the water temples of Bali and Java, going to conferences, publishing more water books. I moved into an office in an old building in Sydney's Chinatown and began to write in earnest, surrounded by my collection of artworks and images of the water deities of many cultures, from the sensuous mermaids of Haitian voodoo to the Celtic Lady of the Lake.

One of these images was a photograph of a bronze statue in the British Museum. A woman sits in a pleated dress that falls to her ankles. Her hair neatly coiffured, her face in repose, she looks every inch an aristocrat; but protruding from the rear of her dress is a long naked fish tail similar to those of the bottom dwelling fish we call 'flathead'.

She is a woman fish. Her name is Damkina, Queen of the Waters, a 4000-year-old Goddess from Mesopotamia. Revered by early humans because they inhabited the abyssal womb of the Great Ocean Mother, fish were associated with hidden mysteries and secrets their eyes alone had witnessed. Fish, like Gods, never close their eyes. Like Gods, they see everything. Theirs is the wisdom of the deep.

Peruvian creation stories tell of the holy fish named Heaven, who was mother of all. In India Vishnu in his fish incarnation saved the world from destruction.

Among the Chaldeans a magic fish with the head of a swallow signified cyclic regeneration, a concept eventually incorporated into Pisces, the twelfth sign of the Zodiac, the ancient calendar of the astrologers of Babylon. A Babylonian seal from 700 BC shows fish gods fertilising the Tree of Life; in another, a fish deity holds an urn from which other fish emerge. The priests of the fish gods are wrapped in cloaks that imitate the split body of a fish; the head had its mouth open to the sky, crowning its wearer. This unusual headgear became the mitre worn by Christian bishops, whose original symbol was not a cross but a fish.

The Greek philosopher Anaximander of Miletus taught that in the creative beginning 'strange fish were generated by the warming of earth and ocean. Inside these, human beings developed, remaining in the fish until they reached puberty. Then the first men and women broke open their host fishes and stepped out onto the earth'. The veneration of fish gods as conduits for the wisdom of the deep reached its peak in Akkad between 2000 and 3000 BC, where the principal deities were Oannes, Lord of the Waters and Damkina, she with the flathead tail. The kingdom of Akkad between the Tigris and Euphrates Rivers, had its capital at Eridu on the Persian Gulf. When their civilisation declined, the priests of the fish cult moved to Babylon with the magic books and scriptures of Akkad which were preserved as holy relics. The Akkadian speech was retained as a sacred language, much as Latin was by Catholics.

Thus it is that the only description of Oannes survives in a text written by Berossus, a priest at the Temple of Bel in 300 BC.

> In the first year there made its appearance from a part of the Erythrean sea, an animal endowed with reason, who was called Oannes. The whole body of the animal was like that of a fish; and had under a fish's head another head, and also feet below, similar to those of a man, subjoined to the fish's tail. His voice, too, and language were articulate and human; and a representation of him is preserved to this day. This Being in the daytime used to converse with men; but took no food at that season; and he gave them an insight into letters and sciences, and every kind of art. He taught them to construct houses, to find temples, to compile laws, and explained to them the principles of geometrical knowledge. He made them distinguish the seeds of the earth, and showed them how to collect fruits; in short, he instructed them in

everything which could tend to soften manners and humanise mankind. From that time, so universal were his instructions, nothing material has been added by way of improvement. When the sun set, it was the custom of this Being to plunge again into the sea and abide all night in the deep.

Another wise man of the sea appears in the migration stories of North American Indians who came from Kamchatka and Siberia across the Bering Straits ten or twenty thousand years ago.

The ancestors of the Shawano nation once lived across the Great Salt Lake in a land of frost, snow and icy wind. In spring when the weather was warmer, people camped on the shore gathering shellfish and hunting for seals. Suddenly, out of the sea came a strange creature that made even the bravest warriors flee in terror.

His long green hair resembled sea grass, his face was that of a dolphin with a beard the colour of slime. Around his neck hung a necklace of shells; a string of white crocodile teeth held back his hair. In his hand he held a staff made from the rib of a whale. When this being emerged from the water, the people saw that below the waist his body divided into two fishtails. He began to speak, calling to them in their language, but they were afraid. Abandoning camp, the group fled into the forest. The shamans decided that this was a benevolent spirit so everyone returned to hear what he had to say. The creature sang of the wonders beneath the ocean, and of a land of sunshine and abundance on the other side of the Great Salt Lake. This paradise awaited the Shawanos, he said, and he was sent to guide them. His offer was respectfully declined but each spring the spirit being returned to sing his songs and tell his stories.

Then came the great famine. The fish and game and seals disappeared; children died of starvation and there was much sadness. This time when the fish spirit repeated his invitation, the Shawanos decided to follow him. Loading their canoes, they set out in great fear, passing through terrible storms and wild seas— and always the spirit remained with them, singing, lifting up their hearts, urging them on. They travelled for two and a half moons until the weather became warmer, the seas calmer. Then, on the horizon, land, shining in the sun as the spirit had promised. They paddled to the shore where seals played among the rocks. Beyond, lay forests alive with game and rivers teeming with salmon and wild duck. The grateful Shawanos enshrined the ocean spirit in their hearts and told his story often in their teepees.

'My soul is full of longing for the secret of the sea,' sings Henry Longfellow, 'and the heart of the great ocean sends a thrilling pulse through me.'

Why does the ocean inspire such poetic expressions of passion, love and longing that, in spite of our rational selves, we are moved with emotion?

'I have loved thee Ocean!' declares Lord Byron, in his exuberant and highly personal celebration of childhood intimacy with the waves.

Each breaking wave is an explosion of energy, a glorious fusion of air, light and water, one following another in an infinite procession that invites us to join their eternal dance.

Surfers worship waves. They, more than most, are intimately acquainted with the sea's many moods. Professional surfers have their own sacred language to describe the subtle nuances of waves. Baffling to the uninitiated, it speaks of shore breaks, beach breaks, point breaks, reef breaks, peaks, sections, lefts, rights, lines, sets, tunnels, bowls, shoulders, lips, backs, troughs, curls, swells, slop, slosh, glass, juice and tubes.

The wave is a temple; a holy place where surfers go to meet their Maker. 'God is a tube,' writes Amélie Nothomb in her *Metaphysics of the Tubes*. Surfers talk of orgasmic experiences, of revelations, of glimpses of infinity, of the ephemeral beauty of the ocean in motion and the strange fleeting light they call the Eye of God. 'Spiritual metaphors' said one, 'are the only words powerful enough to describe the magic of the waves.'

'Waves,' my grandfather told me with the air of one imparting secret knowledge, 'waves are the nine blonde daughters of Ran, the Norwegian Goddess of the Sea—and the ninth wave is always the most powerful. It makes the loudest roar because it is the voice of the eldest daughter.'

We made sandcastles for the children of Ran to play with, but they just knocked them down and ran away. I spent a lot of time counting waves, trying to find the eldest. I frolicked in the surf with Ran's daughters, and got to know them better and more intimately than real live girls of which there were few in my life at that time.

I'm older now but I still think of the children of the Ocean Goddess, in the light of the wisdom of Lao Tzu.

> To find the origin,
> trace back the manifestations;
> When you recognise the children
> and find the mother
> you will be free from sorrow.

The rhythm of the waves is nature's heartbeat that comforts and nourishes us just as the warmth of a mother's embrace soothes the troubled child.

It is no coincidence that the French words for sea and mother, 'mer' and 'mère', are so intimately connected, as is the old English 'mère' meaning a lake or large body of water. And from this, of course, we have the much beloved 'mer maid', the bare-breasted handmaiden of the sea.

The waves are her caress.

The first mermaids to appeal to the popular imagination were the Nereides who lived in the Aegean Sea and the surrounding Mediterranean. These were the daughters of Nereus, the Old Man of the Sea and grey-eyed Doris, the daughter of Oceanus. Fifty graceful nymphs with enticing voices and bodies that inspired artists, sculptors and poets for centuries.

In his *Natural History* (50 AD), Pliny the Elder seems quite convinced of their existence. 'And as for the Mermaids called Nereides, it is no fabulous tale that goeth of them, for looke how painters draw them, so they are indeed: only their bodie is rough and skaled all over, even in those parts wherein they resemble women.' The ability of the Nereides to stir up storms or calm the waves so impressed Greek sailors and fishermen that altars were erected in their honour all along the coast so that offerings could be made before people went to sea.

Perhaps it was a Nereide that caused such a stir in the tiny Cornish fishing village of Zennor in the fourteenth century. Something strange certainly happened there. No-one knows exactly what. All that remains is a 500-year-old story told around Cornish fireplaces on cold winter nights. In a strange reversal of the siren legend, it tells of a mermaid who was enchanted by the voice of a human.

One of the highlights of the weekly church service at Zennor back then was the performance of the choir. The exquisite voice of young Matthew Trewhalla, son of the local church warden, drew many admirers from far and wide. Carried by the wind, his song was heard by a mermaid far out at sea. Seeking the source of the melody she swam up a stream which flowed beside the church and hid, listening among the willow fronds which overhung the water. When the service was over, Matthew went to the stream to drink. Instead of his own reflection, he saw a beautiful woman smiling up at him beneath the water.

Looking back over her shoulder she turned and swam downstream. Overcome with desire and amazement, Matthew plunged into the water to follow her and vanished, never to be seen again. For years thereafter, people said, his voice could be heard in Pendower Cove as he serenaded his mermaid bride beneath the waves.

Their union appears to have been happy and productive. Ten years after Matthew's disappearance, the captain of a ship moored off Pendower Cove heard a mermaid calling. She had a problem, she said. The heavy ship's anchor had fallen across the entrance to her home preventing her from returning to Matthew and their children. The captain lifted the anchor, and returned to port with his story. In the following year, the folk of Zennor had a craftsman carve the figure of the mermaid on the end of the pew where Matthew had once sat.

In 1952 O.W. Schreiber, a researcher at a United States Navy underwater listening post in Hawaii sat patiently recording the sounds of the sea. He was astonished to hear a series of repetitive moans and high-pitched sounds repeated in regular patterns. Mystified, Schreiber sent the tapes to an oceanographic institute in Massachusetts where the eerie tune was finally identified. It was the first recorded song of a humpback whale.

Since then the haunting underwater melodies of whales have been studied and documented. A recording of *The Songs of the Humpback Whales* spent several weeks in the best-seller charts in the 1970s.

These could well be the fabled songs of sirens and mermaids, says whale expert Roger Payne. 'I've long suspected that the sailors' stories of the sirens had their origins in humpback whale songs,' he writes in *Among Whales*. When the song vibrates through the hull of a wooden boat, 'sounds are being broadcast at you from all points of the hull. Essentially you are sitting in the middle of the loudspeaker with sound coming at you from all directions simultaneously. This is, for any human being, ancient or modern, an entirely unique experience.'

In his book on animal communication, *The Dolittle Obsession*, biologist Michael Bright explains that 'Humpback songs consist of long, complicated, repetitive sequences, much like bird song except that each one can last from five to more than 30 minutes. A whale may start, stop, or resume singing at any point in a song, so it is difficult to determine the beginning, middle and end. Each song is sung over and over again without breaks, except for short breathing spells, for many hours. A whale recorded in the West Indies by Howard and Lois Winn of the University of Rhode Island, sang non-stop for 22 hours!'

We don't know what the whales are singing about so enthusiastically, but we do know that the songs are only heard during the mating season and they're only sung by males. I have a compact disc of these enigmatic melodies. Listening with my eyes closed, I think that perhaps those old sailors were right after all. These are the ancient arias of the Nereides—the love songs of the immortal sea.

# The Dewdrop
# on the Corn

Through many years,
At great expense,
Journeying through many countries,
I went to see high mountains,
I went to see oceans.
Only I had not seen
At my very doorstep,
The dew drop glistening
On the ear of the corn.

Rabindranath Tagore

We do not have to travel far to connect with the wisdom of water. It is ever-present within us and without. In the midst of every great metropolis dew still drops and rain still falls. Even the water flowing from our kitchen taps carries messages from distant springs and mountains reminding us that we are all one.

Find time if you can to sit quietly beside a river and absorb its power and energy. 'The flow of wisdom is as continuous and unstoppable as the current of a mighty river,' the sage Padmasambhava tells us. 'Look into your own mind to know whether or not this is true.'

When we begin to commune with nature and affirm our connection with the divinity inherent in all things, meanings and significances will appear that were previously invisible to us. When each rock and tree and stream, even the most minute drop of dew feels like family, we know we are no longer alone.

Don't wait too long.

We are only here because water has chosen Earth as a playground for a while.

When she leaves so will we.

# Acknowledgements

*The Wisdom of Water* is another milestone in an adventure that began long ago and far away. It has, for the most part, been a journey in the company of women without whose inspiration, enthusiasm and support I could not have come this far.

In respect of this particular work I owe much to Bridget Ninness who patiently converted my hand-written manuscript into type, offered frank and fearless critical input and created the cover artwork.

Zora Marresh, spiritual elder and custodian of Sydney's Adyar Library often lit the path in times of darkness, ably assisted by Louise Proudman. Maya Verma and Sophie Pearce provided invaluable research assistance, and Patricia Durban lent me her hideaway on the Hawkesbury River to escape to when I needed another perspective.

The team at Allen & Unwin have been a delight to work with. I would particularly like to thank Carolyn Crowther for leading me to their door, publisher Maggie Hamilton for her vision, her contagious enthusiasm and unfailing optimism and Siobhán Cantrill for her meticulous attention to detail and patient good humour.

And watching over all is Tramerag, the angel of the mist.

Thank you all for everything.